PRE-CUT COMBO Quilts

14 quilts that blend jelly rolls,
layer cakes, turnovers and more

DEBRA FEHR GREENWAY

KRAUSE PUBLICATIONS
CINCINNATI, OHIO

Table of Contents

Introduction

My brother and fellow author, Dennis, told me that writers pen the introduction to their books last, right before the book goes to press. I'm glad I followed that wise advice because from the inception of this book until now when I am (finally!) wrapping it up, I have turned some major corners. The original introduction would never have cut it.

When I first got the idea to write a book about combining multiple sizes and cuts of pre-cut fabrics, that's about all I had in mind. For years I had worked in quilt shops, and I can't count how many customers would actually caress the pre-cuts and tell me how they would love to have all of them—they just didn't know what to use them for! I was empathetic, to say the least. I had always tried to use just about every fabric in any given line for the dozens of store samples I made. So I started to play with combining pre-cuts, and that's where it all began. PRE-CUTS POTPOURRI (page 94) is one of the first of these quilts (it made a really fun class, too). WONKY POSIES (page 10), GREAT BOUNCING BEGONIAS (page 42), LAYER CAKE CHARM (page 66), CHRISTMAS BLESSING (page 110) and the cover quilt, LOG CABIN SCHOOLHOUSE (page 72), were all made in the early stages of playing with pre-cuts—experimenting with appliqué, prairie points, paper piecing and various settings.

I know how popular printed panels are and realized that these cuties are a natural to use in conjunction with pre-cuts. They became easy to use when I found that by varying the size of inner border yardages I could easily surround the panels with pre-cut borders that fit perfectly! RUDOLPH'S ENCOURAGEMENT COMMITTEE (page 104) is a great example of this technique.

Fairly soon into this process, I realized that because many manufacturers use the same dyes in their fabric lines, I could combine pre-cuts from different lines. NOT THE OLD-SCHOOL WAY (page 88) uses two lines of pre-cuts from two different Moda designers. From there, it was not a stretch to try using batik pre-cuts with solids, as in HOLLYHOCKS (page 50) and MIXED FRUIT SORBET (page 58). Mixing pre-cuts got a whole lot more fun, and the opportunities for design exploded.

By far though, the most exciting and explosive innovation was when I figured out a way to use fat quarter bundles for pre-cuts. Now I could move way beyond the restriction of which manufacturers made pre-cuts and explore other manufacturers that made fat quarter bundles. MOTHER OF PEARL (page 26) is one such quilt, as are the BIG BROTHER'S QUILT and KID SISTER'S QUILT pair (pages 100–103). The latter two are examples of one fat quarter bundle divided by color to make coordinating quilts. What fun!

Then lo and behold, I realized I could make up my own fat quarter bundles! Now, truly, the sky was the limit. I bundled up some hand-dyed fabrics for HOT SUMMER DAZE (page 117), POP, SIZZLE, BLOOM! (page 22) and THE FALL OF AUTUMN (page 119), all of which sprang from this idea.

I knew I had to include a fat quarter (or fat eighth) cutting diagram for every pattern. This way, your opportunities are also unlimited. And I can write my introduction in peace, knowing that I have truly made an effort to split the pre-cuts field wide open! I hope you enjoy these patterns, and I would love to see every quilt you make from them.

Quilt, bind and enjoy!

Pre-Cuts: Basics + Beyond

I remember (much too well) cutting piecing templates from plastic milk cartons. That was my big contribution to recycling in the 1980s! Do any of you remember the rotary cutter revolution? It was amazing and instrumental in spurring on the incredible quilting explosion of that decade.

I can't say that pre-cuts will change the quilting world the way the rotary experience did, but I can say that pre-cuts are one of the handiest innovations since. First we had fat quarters, then charm squares, and from there we received a plethora of additions to the family. The depth of this movement is yet to be determined, as it is limited only by the creative minds of those who market them—from the local shop owner to the big guys in manufacturing.

As quilters continue to create, the market for pre-cuts and their applications will continue to grow. Recently I was able to purchase a whole set of 2½" squares. So keep your eyes peeled!

TYPES OF PRE-CUTS

The fat quarter, fat eighth and sweet sixteens are all cuts based on fractions of yardage. These three types of pre-cuts are user-friendly and have many applications. Many times you can find these pre-cuts bundled by entire fabric lines. Many shops will bundle and sell pleasing assortments, but you can also find them individually to make up your own assortment.

- Fat quarters are 18" wide × 22" long—twice the length and half the width of a quarter yard. They always have one selvage edge.

- Fat eighths are 9" wide × 22" long, including a selvage edge.

- Sweet sixteens are fairly new on the market and run half the size of a fat eighth—about 9" wide × 11" long.

Layer cakes, jelly rolls, charm squares, honey buns, dessert rolls and turnovers are sets of fabric that have specific common dimensions. When the manufacturer bundles them up, they usually come as an entire fabric line, varying from about twelve to maybe forty-four fabrics.

- Layer cakes are 10" squares.

- Jelly rolls are 2½" strips × Width of Fabric (WoF, 40–44").

- Charm squares are usually 5" squares, but vary from source to source (in the past, 6" squares were common).

- Honey buns are 1½" wide × WoF.

- Dessert rolls usually contain all the solids and/or tone-on-tones in a fabric line and are 5" wide × WoF.

- Turnovers are 6" half-square triangles, which can be sewn together and trimmed down to 5" squares.

WORKING WITH PRE-CUTS

Every manufacturer seems to have a different kind of edge—some are straight and some are ziggy-zaggy, pinked edges to help prevent raveling. Where in all of that are you supposed to place a ¼" seam allowance? There is a pretty easy solution: measure. Don't take anything for granted. See for yourself where the seamline has to be to make a perfect 2" jelly roll seam, or where you need to place the charm square by your needle to get a dead-on 4½" square.

Subcutting pre-cuts seems to be another bugaboo. For instance, sometimes I will use charm squares for sashing corner squares by cutting them into four equal 2½" squares. Where do you cut? Many times the point of the pinked edge is the correct spot to line up with the straight edge of a rotary-cut piece, but please don't take that for granted. If you measure your pre-cuts like I mentioned above, you will know where to cut. Then, if you have to stitch a pinked edge to a straight-cut edge, you will know where to align them.

Turnovers have a long bias edge that is very easy to stretch out of shape. Please be very gentle with turnovers. When you are sewing any bias edge to a straight edge, the rule of thumb is to place the bias edge on the bottom. You may choose to pin it, too, but it almost always will feed right in with no problems.

Now that you know these few easy tips, your results will be consistent and accurate. With any luck at all, you will become as addicted to pre-cuts as I am!

UNIQUE USES FOR PRE-CUTS

Pre-cuts aren't just for piecing. I have discovered how handy they are to use in many different applications! Here are some of my favorites:

- Jelly rolls make the coolest scrappy bindings. Already cut at 2½" wide, you may use any of your leftover jelly roll strips to make a perky, scrappy binding for your quilt. If you don't have enough for the entire binding, you may incorporate some other scraps. Jelly rolls are also handy for my second favorite application, sashing. You usually have enough left over from the sashing to also do the binding, and if you don't, a few pieces of scrap yardage make up the difference.

- I love to appliqué and have found that pre-cuts are a nice size to start with. It's so easy to run into a shop and grab a package of pre-cuts for your appliqués and have all you need right there. Who really wants to shop for a couple dozen ⅛ yard cuts?

- Paper piecing is another natural for pre-cuts. My wall quilt, *CHRISTMAS BLESSING* (page 110), is a good example of using pre-cuts for all of those little pieces. Just like in appliqué, it's so much easier to use pre-cuts than shop for all of those pieces individually.

- The cover quilt, *LOG CABIN SCHOOLHOUSE* (page 72), was my first experience using charm squares to make prairie points. What can I say? All I did was fold and sew!

- Layer cake squares make good, plain alternate blocks, but they are also fabulous for embroidery and appliqué backgrounds. I love printed backgrounds, and it is so nice to find just the right one all pre-cut and ready in the same fabrics you are using for the rest of the project.

USE UP THE LEFTOVERS AND MAKE FABRIC

Leftovers—what can you create with them that is new and exciting? I have had the same dilemma in the sewing room as in the kitchen. But leftover pre-cuts are just plain fun!

I don't know how many patterns are out there for pillow cases, purses, totes, children's wear, aprons, wallets, and on and on and on. I do know that these patterns are great for using leftovers from the projects in this book. Plus, with the employ of a few choice brain cells, you can think up your own patterns!

One thing I love to do with leftover pre-cuts is "make fabric." I did this in making the appliqué fabric for the flowers in *GREAT BOUNCING BEGONIAS* (page 42). The easiest way to make fabric is to join like sizes of pre-cuts together. For instance, you can sew a row of ten charm squares to make a strip of fabric, and then expand on it by stitching it to jelly roll or honey bun strips, or both. This is a fun way to come up with enough yardage to cut a vest front, a purse or even a doll quilt.

I love to make pillow cases for my quilts. Some of my quilt patterns end up with an extra block or two. These blocks are easily framed with pre-cut strips. Add extra border fabrics for a great background and edging, and you have a pillow top. Extra blocks are also great for tote bag pockets. It seems I always overbuy backing, and that extra yardage is wonderful for pillow backs, vest backs, and purse or tote bag linings.

So go for it! Have fun with your leftovers. You needed a new wallet anyway, and that canvas bag you want to make is just crying out for some scrappy, three-dimensional *WONKY POSIES* (page 10), isn't it?

HARMONIOUSLY COMBINE PRE-CUTS

Looking at a bundle of pre-cuts can be a little intimidating. I have heard people say that all the fabrics just blend together and there is no contrast. I can appreciate their sentiment and have at times stewed over this myself. However, after working with so many of them, I have noticed that with almost any given line of fabric, the manufacturer includes an assortment of very large focus and/or border prints, medium and small prints, and tone-on-tone or solid fabrics, sometimes in several colorways. The key to making sense of it all is to open up the bundles of pre-cuts and sort them out accordingly. Then you will be able to see that, sure enough, there are darks and lights, solids and prints!

Another invaluable tool I have used in this book is combining a typical line of printed pre-cuts with a package of pre-cuts that is completely made up of solids, even if they're not from the same manufacturer. This works fabulously, and you can see the results in *MIXED FRUIT SORBET* (page 58). You can also combine two different lines of print pre-cuts from the same manufacturer because the dyes they use are often similar. I did this with *NOT THE OLD-SCHOOL WAY* (page 88). Can you tell?

We all know that fabric manufacturers are prolific in their output, and any line of fabrics may be available for only a very short while. That's okay! I have given specific colors in the pattern text for easy reference to the project photos and diagrams, but feel free to use any colors you want. I even made fabric substitution suggestions near the beginning of each pattern. Just use the colors in the text as a reference, and substitute your favorite combinations.

Finally, for the very first time in a book on pre-cuts, I give you the freedom to be the design artist for your very own line of fabric choices! Every pattern in this book offers you the freedom to use either fat quarters or fat eighths in place of pre-cuts. This is particularly handy when you fall in love with a fabric line that does not come in pre-cuts. For instance, when I saw the Stonehenge line of fabrics by Northcott, I could only get pre-cuts in 2½" strips. So I bought a selection of fat eighths to work with it. You can see this approach was perfect for *THE FALLS AT STONE POOL* (page 118).

So go ahead—be creative! The opportunities for your very own take on pre-cuts are now endless!

SHOP WITH CONFIDENCE

You are at a quilt shop days from home and see the perfect pre-cuts for your project. They even have all the coordinating yardage, but how do you know what you need? Through years of making many pre-cut quilts, I have found some standard yardages you may find handy. You may wish to know how much you need down to the inch, but it is not always economical to guess at less and then be stuck on a project because you don't have enough fabric. On the other hand, you don't want to buy 6 yards of everything! Here are some tips to take with you. Stick them in your wallet, and shop for yardage with confidence.

- **Alternate Blocks:** You can get three 14" blocks across the WoF that can easily trim down to size after optional appliqué or embroidery. If you want twelve of these blocks, you need 1½ yards. A light tone-on-tone or solid works best for this.

- **Background Fabric for Piecing:** This is the most difficult to estimate because pieced blocks are so varied from quilt to quilt. If you are making a quilt that is predominantly background, I strongly suggest you check out similar patterns in the shop and see what they suggest. Most pre-cut quilts have limited background, and pre-cut combo quilts even less because you want to include as many pre-cuts as possible. I have found that 2 yards of a light tone-on-tone, solid or subtle print is usually sufficient.

- **Narrow Border:** Most of the time I like to separate the inner quilt top from the wide border with a dark solid, tone-on-tone or tiny print 1" narrow border. This rarely takes more than ½ yard, but I usually buy 1 yard. Five dollars for my peace of mind is usually worth it.

- **Outer Border:** Whenever I can, I like to cut my outer border lengthwise to avoid seaming it. Believe it or not, it doesn't take that much extra yardage. Most borders are not longer than 3 yards, even for a king-size mitered corner. If I'm not mitering the corner on a huge quilt, I can get by with 2½ yards, and 2 yards for throws or crib quilts. When you cut these borders lengthwise, you have the added bonus of being able to use the extra fabric (cut lengthwise also) for binding if you don't mind binding with straight grain fabric. A large print that blends most of the quilt's colors, like a focus fabric or a border print, works best.

- **Binding:** Only the largest quilts take more than a yard of binding fabric. Buy 1½ yards for a king-size quilt and 1 yard for everything smaller. If I am not using leftover outer border fabric, I usually buy a dark solid, tone-on-tone, or a tiny or geometric print.

Now you know that you can shop confidently and buy all you need at one time! If it costs you a little extra money, you can still sleep better at night knowing that you'll have enough fabric to finish your quilt. It seems I always end up using the extra fabric in the blocks anyway. Besides, leftover fabric is amazing for making coordinating totes, pillows and pillow cases, purses, vests, place mats and so much more. And who among us has never bought extra "for the stash"?

I love this fabric! How much should I buy?

- **Alternate Blocks:** Approximately 1½ yards

- **Background Fabric for Piecing:** Approximately 2 yards

- **Narrow Border:** 1 yard

- **Outer Border:** 2 yards (crib/throw), 2½ yards (full/queen/king, not mitered), 3 yards (king, mitered borders)

- **Binding:** 1 yard, 1½ yards (king)

- -

I love this pattern! Which fabric should I buy?

- **Alternate Blocks:** Tone-on-tone or solid

- **Background Fabric for Piecing:** Light tone-on-tone, solid or subtle print

- **Narrow Border:** Dark tone-on-tone, solid or tiny print

- **Outer Border:** Large print or border print to match quilt top interior

- **Binding:** Dark tone-on-tone, solid or tiny print; outer border leftover fabric

Photocopy, cut out and fold to make a reference card to carry in your wallet.

Wonky Posies

How can you look at this quilt and not smile? The ribbon-festooned lattice jumps to life with whimsical posies. These three-dimensional flowers are easy, and the woven trellis frames simple layer cake blocks. It's sure to bring a smile to someone's face!

Quilt Size: 78" × 78" (Twin/Full)

Block Size: 13½" × 13½"

Pieced and quilted by the author.

Choosing Fabrics

I used the *Baskets of Flowers* Moda pre-cut line for this quilt. You may choose pre-cuts that feature primary colors, with a focus on red, chartreuse, pink and white. Or use any line that has similar colors. Purchase additional yardage as specified in colors that coordinate with your particular pre-cut line.

- -

This Quilt's Pre-Cuts...

layer cake • jelly roll •
charm squares • turnover

MATERIALS

FOR PRE-CUTS QUILT

1 layer cake (Blocks and Posies)

1 jelly roll (Block Frames)

(88) 5" charm squares (Posies)

1 turnover (Setting Triangles)

Additional yardage

FOR FAT QUARTER QUILT

1 fat quarter bundle or at least 24 coordinating fat quarters (Blocks, Posies, Frames, Setting Triangles)

Additional yardage

ADDITIONAL YARDAGE

½ yd. red fabric (Inner Border)

2½ yds. striped fabric cut lengthwise or 2 yds. striped fabric cut crosswise (Outer Border)

¾ yd. plaid fabric (Binding)

¼ yd. dark green fabric (Bow Appliqué)

¼ yd. medium green fabric (Bow Appliqué)

¼ yd. dark blue fabric (Bow Appliqué)

¼ yd. medium blue fabric (Bow Appliqué)

BATTING AND BACKING YARDAGE

Double/full size batting

Backing (choose one):

42" wide fabric: 4⅔ yds.
90" wide fabric: 2¼ yds.
108" wide fabric: 2¼ yds.

EXTRA SUPPLIES

1¾ yds. fusible fleece

30 or more 1⅜" brightly colored buttons

Plastic or Mylar template material

Large safety pins

Temporary adhesive spray

Fusible web

Templates (pages 120–121)

CUTTING INSTRUCTIONS

For Fat Quarter Quilt Only

Using the Fat Quarter Cutting Diagram as a guide, cut from each fat quarter:

(2) 2½" wide jelly roll strips.

(1) 6" turnover square. Subcut diagonally corner to corner once.

(1) 10" layer cake square. Set 13 medium-tone prints aside for blocks and subcut the remaining layer cake squares into 5" charm squares.

(3) 5" charm squares.

(1) 2½" wide partial jelly roll strip.

Follow the instructions below for subcutting and sorting pre-cuts.

For Pre-Cuts and Fat Quarter Quilts

From the layer cake, separate out 13 medium-tone prints. They will be used as whole blocks on the quilt and give the eye a place to rest.

From the jelly roll strips:

If using pre-cuts, separate out 13 dark and 13 light strips (Block Frames). Cut each strip into (2) 12" pieces. Set the rest aside (Setting and Corner Triangles).

If using strips cut from fat quarters, set aside 1 full-length strip from each fat quarter (Setting and Corner Triangles). Subcut the remaining full strip and partial strip from each fat quarter to 12" long (Block Frames).

From the turnover triangles, separate out:

8 groups of 4 triangles each, each group containing 2 identical lights and 2 coordinating identical darks (Side Setting Triangles).

4 groups of 2 triangles each, each group containing 1 light and 1 coordinating dark (Corner Setting Triangles).

From the plaid fabric, cut 2½" bias strips for the binding.

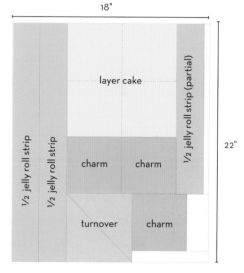

Fat Quarter Cutting Diagram

SEWING INSTRUCTIONS

Layer Cake Blocks (Make 13)

1. Pair up two light and two dark 12" strips for each layer cake square. Mix and match until each block looks pleasing to you.

2. Starting in the upper right corner and with right sides together, sew a dark strip to the layer cake square about halfway across the top. Press the sewn part open. (Figure 1)

3. Sew a light strip down the right side. Press open. (Figure 2)

4. Sew the other light strip across the bottom. Press open. (Figure 3)

5. Sew the other dark strip onto the left side. Press open. (Figure 4)

6. Finish sewing the top dark strip across, overlapping the stitches from the first pass. Press open. (Figures 5 and 6)

7. Lay out these blocks on your design wall according to the Quilt Layout (page 17). Play with the arrangement until it is pleasing to you, noting the positions of dark and light frames.

Setting Triangles (Make 8)

1. Referring to the Quilt Layout for orientation, lay out one set of four turnovers on your sewing table.

2. Sew each dark to its light, noting that the placement of darks and lights must be consistent. Press.

3. Join the two sets together to complete the triangle unit. Press. Repeat to make eight setting triangles. (Figures 7 and 8)

Corner Triangles (Make 4)

1. Referring to the Quilt Layout, lay out a set of two turnovers on your sewing table.

2. Sew the two triangles together to complete the triangle unit. Press open. Repeat to make four corner triangles. (Figure 9)

Figure 1

Figure 2

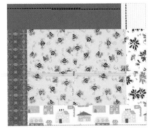

Figure 3

Figure 4

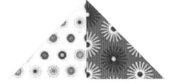

Figure 5

Figure 6

Figure 7

Figure 8

Figure 9

Setting and Corner Triangle Units

1. Lay out the setting and corner triangle units on the design wall along with the framed blocks.

2. Choose one 12" and one 18" jelly roll strip to frame each setting triangle; light jelly roll strips should be placed next to dark-frame blocks, and dark strips next to light-frame blocks. In the same way, choose one 18" jelly roll strip for each corner triangle. Pin each strip to its unit.

3. With right sides together, line up the peak of a setting triangle with the edge of the short framing strip. Sew the strip to the triangle unit. Press open. Do not trim the extra length off the strip. (Figure 10)

4. With right sides together, line up the longer strip with the top end of the setting triangle unit. Sew this strip to the other side. Press open. Do not trim the extra length off the strip. (Figure 11)

5. Fold the strip that you have chosen for a corner triangle in half and mark the center point.

6. With right sides together, match the center point of the strip with the seam on the long edge of the corner triangle. Sew the seam. Press open. Do not trim the extra length off the strip ends. (Figure 12)

ASSEMBLING THE QUILT TOP

1. Using the Quilt Layout as a reference (page 17), lay out the blocks to create color balance across the quilt top. Be careful to watch the orientation of light and dark block frames.

2. Lay out the setting and corner triangles around the four outer sides of the top.

3. Starting in the upper left corner, sew a corner triangle to its adjacent block. Trim the extra length off the framing strip. Press the block open. (Figure 13)

4. Sew a setting triangle to each side of that block. Trim the extra length off the framing strips. Press. (Figure 13)

5. Starting with the next diagonal row, sew the first setting triangle to the first block. Press as you sew. Continue joining the blocks in that row, ending with the final setting triangle.

6. Continue joining blocks in this manner, ending with joining the final corner block.

7. Sew the rows together to complete the inner top.

8. The size of your inner top should now measure 57$\frac{3}{4}$" square.

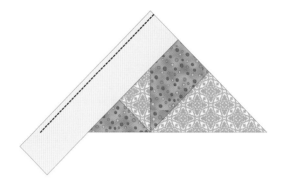

Figure 10

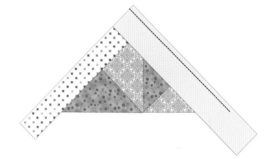

Figure 11

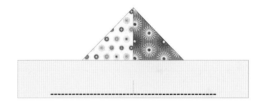

Figure 12

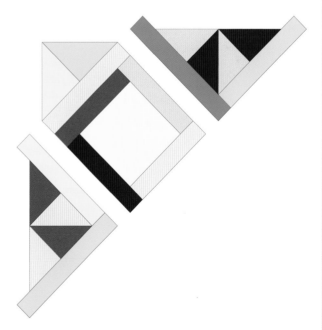

Figure 13

ADDING THE BORDERS

Inner Border

1. From the red Inner Border fabric, cut six 2½" wide strips. Cut two strips in half and sew them to the ends of the other four strips.

2. Cut two of these strips to 57¾" long.

3. With right sides together, sew these two shorter borders to the sides of the quilt. It will be easier to ease in the bias edges of the triangles if you pin every few inches and sew with the border strip on top. Press.

4. Cut the remaining two strips to 61¾" long. In the same way, sew the longer edges to the top and bottom. Press.

5. Your quilt should now measure 61¾" square.

Outer Border (Mitered)

1. For a lengthwise-cut Outer Border, cut four 8½" wide strips by the length of fabric.

2. For a crosswise-cut Outer Border, cut eight 8½" wide strips by the width of fabric. Join each of these strips end-to-end in pairs of two. Press.

3. Fold each border strip to find the middle point and mark it. Likewise, mark the middle point of each side of the quilt top.

4. With right sides together and matching midpoints, sew a border to each side of the quilt. Stop ¼" from the edge of the quilt and backstitch to lock the stitches. Press. (Figure 14)

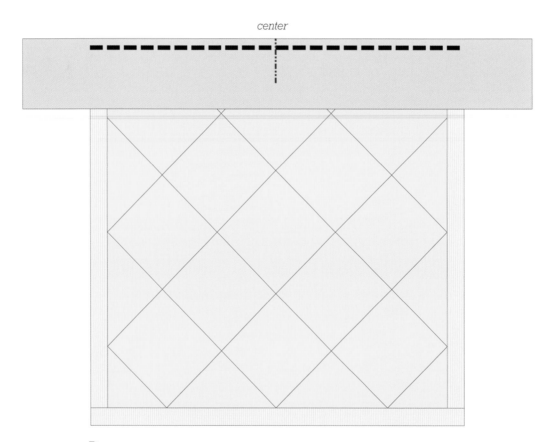

Figure 14

5. Open the borders and lay them out flat, wrong sides up, crossing the strips at the corner. Place a large square ruler on a corner, lining up the outer edges of the border with the outer edges of the ruler. Pin the outer edge of the borders where they cross each other. (Figure 15)

6. Draw a diagonal line from the point where the outer edges cross to the point on the quilt top where the border seamlines end. This will be your seamline. (Figure 16)

7. Fold the quilt in half diagonally, right sides together, lining up the borders. With the drawn diagonal line on top, sew the mitered corner, locking the stitches at both ends. (Figure 17)

8. Trim the excess fabric, leaving a $\frac{1}{4}$" seam allowance. Press. Repeat this process for all four corners. (Figure 18)

9. Your quilt should now measure $77\frac{3}{4}$" square.

ADDING THE APPLIQUÉD BOW

1. Trace the bow templates (page 121) onto your template material. Cut the templates out. Reverse the templates and trace them onto fusible web, leaving about a $\frac{1}{2}$" space between the pieces.

2. Cut out the fusible web, leaving a $\frac{1}{4}$" space around each piece.

3. Fuse the web onto the backs of the two blue and two green bow fabrics, according to the manufacturer's directions.

4. Cut out the fused pieces on the cutting line and remove the paper backing.

5. Carefully place the bow pieces on the quilt referring to the Bow Placement Guide (page 121). When you are pleased with the arrangement, fuse them onto the quilt top.

6. Appliqué stitch around all the edges.

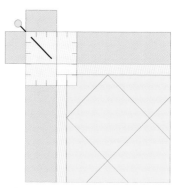

Figure 15

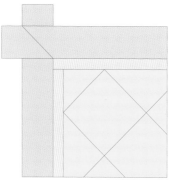

Figure 16

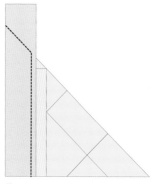

Figure 17

Figure 18

MAKING THE THREE-DIMENSIONAL POSIES

1. Choose forty-four charm squares for the posy tops. Fuse them to the fusible fleece and cut them apart.

2. Choose forty-four more charm squares (or cut scraps of fabric into 5" squares) for the posy backs. Spray the wrong sides of the backs with temporary adhesive spray and attach them to the backs of the fused charm squares.

3. Trace both petal templates (page 120) onto template material. Cut them out.

4. Trace twenty-one large petals and twenty-three small petals onto the top sides of the fused charm squares. Do not cut the petals out.

5. Sew around the edges of the petals, using a very dense satin stitch.

6. Cut out the posies very close to, but not touching, the stitching.

SHAPING THE BORDER

1. Trace the templates for the focus corner and the rounded corners (page 120) onto template material and cut them out.

2. Lining up the rounded corner template with the three plain corners of the quilt, draw the rounded edge directly onto your quilt top with a fine pencil or chalk. This drawn line will be your cutting line. Draw the focus corner template onto the corner with the appliquéd bow.

3. Sandwich and quilt the quilt, choosing a pattern that fits 1/2" inside the markings for the curved corners.

4. Square up your quilt, retracing your corners if you need to. Trim the curved corners on the marked lines.

SEWING THE POSIES TO THE QUILT TOP

1. Arrange the posies across the quilt top using the Quilt Layout as a guide. Some posies will be doubled (layered large and small petals), and some will be only large or small.

2. When you are satisfied with the arrangement, place a button with each posy. Secure it with a large safety pin.

3. Carefully mark the center of each posy placement on the quilt top with a pencil.

4. Make a small pleat in the center of a posy and baste the pleat down on your sewing machine. (This will give it even more "pop" and personality on the quilt top.)

5. Return the posy to the quilt top and layer it as you choose. Place the button on the pleat. Using bobbin thread that matches the backing fabric, sew all layers through the button holes using a large, dense zigzag stitch. Repeat for all posies.

ADDING APPLIQUÉD POSIES

1. You may also choose to appliqué some posies right onto the quilted top. Fuse a charm square for each appliqué to fusible fleece. Trace the posy onto the charm square and cut it out.

2. Spray fusible adhesive to the back of the fleece and adhere the posy to its spot on the quilt top.

3. Appliqué the posy using a very dense satin stitch. A nice bobbin thread makes these posies pretty on the back of your quilt, too!

Bind your quilt and cuddle up!

Alternate Colorway

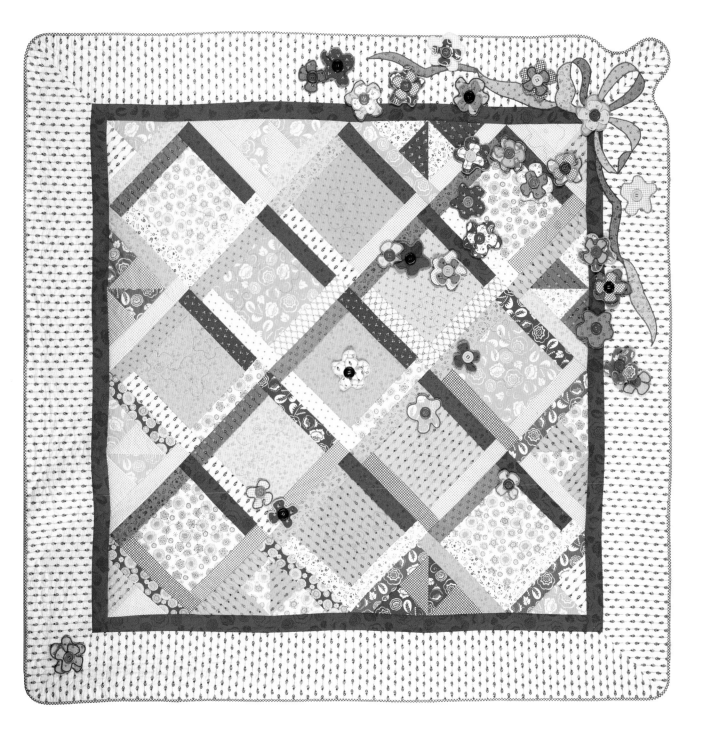

Quilt Layout

Sunkissed

When the spring comes fresh into the garden and kisses the cool soil, flowers burst into bloom. With all its soft colors and simple beauty, this quilt reminds me of that time.

Quilt Size: 81" × 105" (Full with Pillow Tuck)

Block Size: 12" × 12"

Pieced by the author, quilted by Bobbi Lang.

Choosing Fabrics

I used the *Sunkissed* Moda fat eighth bundle for this quilt. If it's not available, choose pre-cuts that feature small, simple prints. Or use any line that has no single overwhelming print. Purchase additional yardage as specified in colors that coordinate with your particular pre-cut line.

- -

This Quilt's Pre-Cuts...

layer cake • honey bun •
charm squares • jelly roll

MATERIALS

FOR PRE-CUTS QUILT

1 layer cake (Blocks)

1 honey bun (Blocks)

(70) 5" charm squares (Blocks)

1 jelly roll (Blocks)

Additional yardage

FOR FAT EIGHTH QUILT

1 fat eighth bundle or at least 40 coordinating fat eighths (Blocks)

(80) 5" charm squares (Blocks)

Additional yardage

ADDITIONAL YARDAGE

³/₄ yd. accent fabric (Borders 1 and 3)

1³/₄ yds. coordinating fabric (Outer Border 4)

⁷/₈ yd. (Binding)

BATTING AND BACKING YARDAGE

King size batting

Backing (choose one):

42" wide fabric: 7¹/₃ yds.
90" wide fabric: 3 yds.
108" wide fabric: 3 yds.

CUTTING INSTRUCTIONS

For Fat Eighth Quilt Only

Using the Fat Eighth Cutting Diagram as a guide, cut from each fat eighth:

(1) 8¹/₂" wide layer cake strip; subcut 1 pile of 8¹/₂" squares.

(2) 2¹/₂" wide jelly roll strips.

(2) 1¹/₂" wide honey bun strips.

Follow the instructions below for subcutting pre-cuts and cutting additional yardage.

For Pre-Cuts and Fat Eighth Quilts

Trim each layer cake square to an 8¹/₂" square.

Cut 1 charm square into (4) 2¹/₂" squares for Border 2. Trim each of the remaining charm squares down to a 4¹/₂" square.

Cut the jelly roll and honey bun strips into 12¹/₂" long strips.

From the accent fabric, cut:

(16) 1¹/₂" strips from the accent fabric for Narrow Border 1 and Narrow Border 3.

(1) 1¹/₂" wide strip; subcut it into (8) 2¹/₂" long pieces for Border 2.

Cut (9) 6¹/₂" strips from the coordinating Outer Border fabric.

Cut 2¹/₂" strips from the binding fabric.

Sew You Know...

I used a fat eighth bundle for this quilt. If you want to use fat quarters, you may use twenty and lay the Cutting Diagram side by side on the fat quarters.

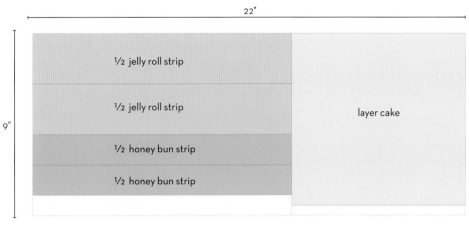

Fat Eighth Cutting Diagram

SEWING INSTRUCTIONS

Blocks (Make 35)

1. For each block, join two coordinating charm squares side by side. Press toward the darker block.

2. Sew an 8½" square to one of the long sides of the charm squares unit. Press toward the large square. (Figure 1)

3. Choose two coordinating honey bun strips and a jelly roll strip that matches one of the honey bun strips. Sew the three strips together with the matching strips on the outsides. Press toward the darker color.

4. Lay the charm/layer cake block out so the charms are on the top. Sew the honey bun side of the step 3 unit to the right side of the block. Press toward the honey bun strip. (Figure 2)

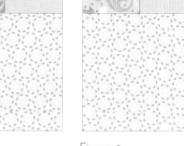

Figure 1   Figure 2

ASSEMBLING THE TOP

1. Using the Quilt Layout (page 21) as a guide, lay out the quilt five blocks across by seven blocks down.

2. Sew the blocks together into rows. Press seams to one side on odd-numbered rows and to the other side on even-numbered rows.

3. Sew the rows together to finish the inner top. Press the seams in one direction.

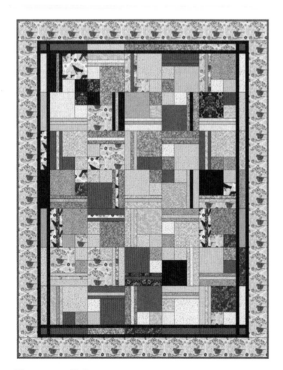

Alternate Colorway

ADDING THE BORDERS

Narrow Border 1

1. Measure the quilt from top to bottom in several places and average the results. Piece and cut two border strips that length. Sew one strip to each side of the quilt. Press the seams toward this border.

2. Measure the quilt from side to side in several places and average the results. Piece and cut two strips that length. Sew these strips to the top and bottom of the quilt. Press the seams toward this border.

Pieced Border 2

1. Piece the remaining jelly roll strips together end-to-end to make two borders with five strips each and two borders with seven strips each.

2. Sew one of the 1½" × 2½" accent fabric strips to each end of the strips.

3. Sew a 2½" square to each end of the top and bottom border strips.

4. Sew the longer strips to the sides of the quilt. Press toward the first border.

5. Sew the shorter strips to the top and bottom of the quilt. Press toward the first border.

Narrow Border 3

Measure and sew border strips the same way you did for Narrow Border 1. Press the seams toward Border 3.

Outer Border 4

Measure and sew border strips the same way you did for Narrow Border 1 using the 6½" border strips. Press the seams toward this border.

Layer and quilt, bind and enjoy!

Quilt Layout

VARIATION:
Pop, Sizzle, Bloom!

It's hot out, but the flower gardens are amazing, and so is this variation of *SUNKISSED* (page 18). Bright colors and hot prints explode all the way into next summer. Enjoy, but grab a lemonade first—you'll need it!

Quilt Size: 82" × 109" (Full with Pillow Tuck)

Block Size: 13½" × 13½"

Fabric: The Rowan Designers at Westminster Fabrics

Pieced by the author, quilted by Bobbi Lang.

Choosing Fabrics

For this quilt I used large prints with contrasting fabrics that read as solids. You could choose large and small prints, or florals and geometrics. You could also choose red prints contrasting with black prints, or any other two-color combination. The choice is yours!

- -

This Quilt's Pre-Cuts...

layer cake • honey bun •
charm squares • jelly roll

MATERIALS

FOR PRE-CUTS QUILT

1 layer cake (Blocks)

1 honey bun (Blocks)

(48) 5" charm squares (Blocks) or
(80) 5" charm squares (with Optional
Pieced Border 2)

1 jelly roll (Blocks)

Additional yardage

FOR FAT QUARTER QUILT

1 fat quarter bundle or at least 30
fat quarters (Blocks and Border 2)

Additional yardage

ADDITIONAL YARDAGE

1 yd. accent fabric (Borders 1
and 3)

2 yds. coordinating fabric (Outer
Border 4)

⁷⁄₈ yd. (Binding)

BATTING AND BACKING YARDAGE

King size batting

Backing (choose one):

42" wide fabric: 7¼ yds.

90" wide fabric: 3¼ yds.

108" wide fabric: 3¼ yds.

CUTTING INSTRUCTIONS

For Fat Quarter Quilt Only

Using the Fat Quarter Cutting Diagram as a
guide, cut from each fat quarter:

(1) 10" wide layer cake strip; subcut 1 pile of 9½"
squares and 4 piles of 5" charm squares.

(2) 2½" wide jelly roll strips.

(2) 1" wide honey bun strips.

Follow the instructions below for subcutting
pre-cuts and cutting additional yardage.

For Pre-Cuts and Fat Quarter Quilts

Trim each layer cake square to a 9½" square.

Cut each pre-cut jelly roll strip in half, resulting in
21" strips. Subcut a 14" strip from each of them. Set
the remaining 7" aside for Optional Border 2.

Trim the honey bun strips down to 1" wide; cut
each pre-cut honey bun strip in half, resulting in 21"
strips. Subcut a 14" strip from each of them. Set the
remaining 7" aside for Optional Border 2.

From the accent fabric, cut:

(7) 1½" strips for Border 1.

(8) 2½" strips for Border 3.

Cut (9) 6½" strips from the coordinating Outer
Border fabric.

Cut 2½" strips from the binding fabric.

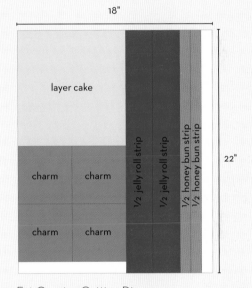

Fat Quarter Cutting Diagram

SEWING INSTRUCTIONS

Blocks (Make 24)

1. For each block, join a solid to a print charm square. Press toward the darker block. (Figure 1)

2. Sew a 9½" square that matches one of those charms to one of the long sides of the charm squares unit so the matching charm is on the left. Press toward the large square. (Figure 2)

3. Choose a 1" × 14" strip that matches the large square and two identical 2½" × 14" jelly roll strips that match the solid charm. Sew the three strips together with the 1" strip in the center. Press toward the darker color. (Figure 3)

4. Lay the charm/layer cake block out so the charms are on the top. Sew the strip unit to the left side of the block. Press toward the strip. (Figure 4)

ASSEMBLING THE TOP

1. Using the Quilt Layout (page 25) as a guide, lay out the quilt four blocks across by six blocks down.

2. Sew the blocks together into rows. Press seams to one side on odd-numbered rows and to the other side on even-numbered rows.

3. Sew the rows together to finish the inner top. Press the seams in one direction.

ADDING THE BORDERS

Narrow Border 1

1. Measure the quilt from top to bottom in several places and average the results. Piece together and cut two border strips that length. Sew one strip to each side of the quilt. Press the seams toward this border.

2. Measure the quilt from side to side in several places and average the results. Piece and cut two more strips that length. Sew these strips to the top and bottom of the quilt. Press the seams toward this border.

Optional Pieced Border 2

1. Gather together all remaining charm squares and 8" leftovers from the jelly roll and honey bun.

2. Assemble strip sets as you did in step 3 of the Block Sewing Instructions. Trim the strip sets to 5" squares.

3. Alternating the strip squares with the charm squares, sew them together end-to-end until you have enough to make borders.

4. Measure the quilt as you did for Narrow Border 1 and cut the pieced strips accordingly. Sew them to the quilt as you did for Narrow Border 1.

Border 3 and Outer Border 4

Measure and sew border strips the same way you did for Narrow Border 1. Press the seams away from the pieced border.

Layer and quilt, bind and enjoy!

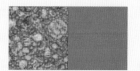

Figure 1

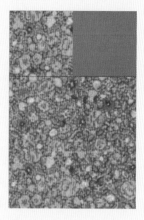

Figure 2

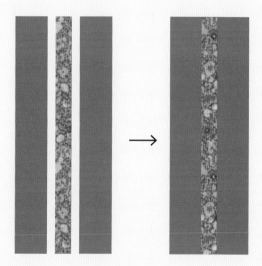

Figure 3

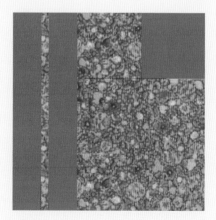

Figure 4

Mother of Pearl

When I saw this package of fat quarters, I knew I was in for a treat! In keeping with the gentle tones, I decided a simple quilt pattern would best enhance the fabrics' soft effect. Four Patches within Four Patches keep the eye moving. Occasional dark spots add a splash of surprise. Enjoy this simple treat!

Quilt Size: 59" × 75" (Throw)

Block Size: 8" × 8"

Pieced and quilted by Susan Wozniak.

Choosing Fabrics

I used a Robert Kaufman *Island Batiks* fat quarter bundle for this quilt. You may choose any coordinated grouping of softly blended, light neutrals with one or two stronger coordinates thrown in, like the dark olive in my quilt. Purchase additional yardage as specified in colors that coordinate with your particular pre-cut line.

- -

This Quilt's Pre-Cuts...

honey bun • charm squares •
jelly roll • layer cake

MATERIALS

FOR PRE-CUTS QUILT

1 honey bun (Blocks)

(38) 5" charm squares* (Blocks)

1 jelly roll (Blocks)

1 layer cake (Blocks)

Additional yardage

*If you want Four Patch blocks with matching alternate squares, purchase 19 identical pairs of charm squares.

FOR FAT QUARTER QUILT

1 fat quarter bundle or at least 18 fat quarters (Blocks)

Additional yardage

ADDITIONAL YARDAGE

⅓ yd. accent fabric (Narrow Border)

2 yds. coordinating fabric (Outer Border and Binding)

BATTING AND BACKING YARDAGE

Twin size batting

Backing (choose one):

42" wide fabric: 3½ yds.
90" wide fabric: 1¾ yds.
108" wide fabric: 1⅝ yds.

CUTTING INSTRUCTIONS

For Fat Quarter Quilt Only

Using the Fat Quarter Cutting Diagram as a guide, cut from each fat quarter:

(2) 2½" wide jelly roll strips. Subcut 8 of the 22" strips into (58) 2½" squares. Set them aside for Unit D.

(1) 1½" wide honey bun strip.

(1) 10" wide layer cake strip; subcut 1 pile of 8½" squares.

Cut the remainder of the 10" fabric strip into (2) 4½" charm square strips; subcut this strip into 3 sets of 4½" squares.

Follow the instructions below for subcutting pre-cuts and cutting additional yardage.

For Pre-Cuts Quilts Only

Trim each layer cake square to an 8½" square.

Subcut 4 of the jelly roll strips into (58) 2½" squares. Label them for Block D.

Trim each charm square to a 4½" square.

For Pre-Cuts and Fat Quarter Quilts

Cut (6) 1½" strips from the accent fabric for the Narrow Border. Cut 12" off 2 of those strips. Pair each of the cut pieces with a whole strip.

From the coordinating Outer Border fabric, cut lengthwise:

(4) 4½" strips for the outer border.

(5) 2½" strips for the binding.

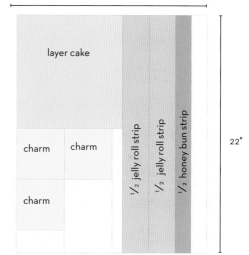

Fat Quarter Cutting Diagram

Strip Piecing Four Patches

1. Sew the long edge of two contrasting fabrics with right sides together. Press toward the darker fabric. (Figure A)

2. Crosscut the strips into units the width of the strips before they were pieced. For example, if you started with $1\frac{1}{2}$" strips, you would subcut the units $1\frac{1}{2}$" wide. (Figure B)

3. Pair up each unit with a matching unit. Turn one upside down and sew it to the other to make the Four Patch block. Press. (Figure C)

Square Piecing Four Patches

1. Make Four Patches by pairing up two squares each of two contrasting fabrics. (Figure D)

2. Sew each pair of squares to its coordinate and press the seams toward the darker fabric. (Figure E)

3. Turn one pair upside down and join it to its partner to make the Four Patch block. Press. (Figure F)

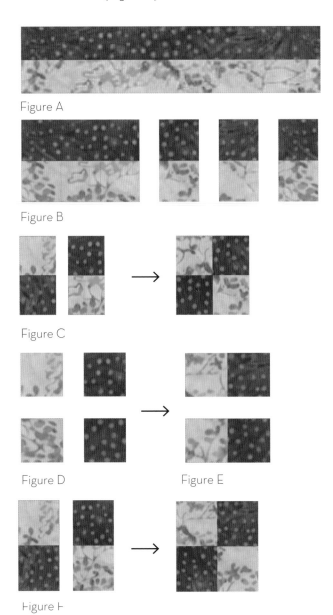

Figure A

Figure B

Figure C

Figure D

Figure E

Figure F

SEWING INSTRUCTIONS

Four Patch Blocks

Block A (Make 58)
From the honey bun strips, make fifty-eight Four Patches using the Strip Piecing Method (page 28). Trim to 2½" square.

Block B (Make 53)
From the jelly roll strips, make fifty-three Four Patches using the Strip Piecing Method (page 28). Trim to 4½" square.

Figure 1

Block C (Make 6)
From the charm squares, make six Four Patch blocks using the Square Piecing Method (page 28). Trim to 8½" square.

Ten Patch Blocks

Block D (Make 29)
1. Gather twenty-nine identical pairs of 2½" squares and the fifty-eight Block A Four Patches.

2. Make twenty-nine Ten Patch blocks by joining two identical squares with two A blocks. Watch the orientation of the A blocks carefully. Trim to 4½" square. (Figure 1)

Figure 2

Block E (Make 7)
1. Gather seven identical pairs of 4½" charm squares and seven identical pairs of Block B Four Patches.

2. Make seven Ten Patch blocks by joining two charm squares with two B blocks. Watch the orientation of the blocks carefully. Trim to 8½" square. (Figure 2)

Sixteen Patch Blocks

Block F (Make 2)
1. Gather eight miscellaneous Block B Four Patches.

2. Make two Sixteen Patch blocks by randomly joining the blocks in sets of four using the Square Piecing Method (page 28). Trim to 8½" square. (Figure 3)

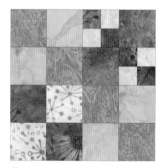

Figure 3

Twenty-Two Patch Block

Block G (Make 1)
1. Gather one Block D Ten Patch and three Block B Four Patches.

2. Make a Twenty-Two Patch block by joining the B and D blocks using the Square Piecing Method (page 28). Watch the orientation of the D block carefully. Trim to 8½" square. (Figure 4)

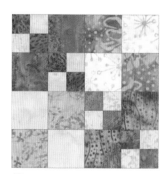

Figure 4

Twenty-Eight Patch Blocks

Block H (Make 14)
1. Gather twenty-eight Block B Four Patches and twenty-eight Block D Ten Patches.

2. Make fourteen Twenty-Eight Patch blocks by joining the B and D units using the Square Piecing Method (page 28). Watch the orientation of the blocks carefully. Trim to 8½" square. (Figure 5)

Figure 5

ASSEMBLING THE TOP

1. Using the Quilt Layout (page 31) as a guide, lay out the quilt six blocks across by eight blocks down.

2. Sew your blocks together into rows. Press your seams to one side on odd-numbered rows and to the other side on even-numbered rows.

3. Sew your rows together to finish the inner top. Press the seams in one direction.

NARROW BORDER

1. Sew each cut border piece to a whole strip.

2. Measure the quilt from top to bottom in several places. Average the results and cut two border strips that length. Sew one strip to each side of the quilt. Press the seams toward this border.

3. Measure the quilt again from side to side in several places. Average the results and cut the remaining two border strips that length. Sew these strips to the top and bottom of the quilt. Press the seams toward this border.

OUTER BORDER

Repeat the Narrow Border steps to sew the Outer Border.

Layer and quilt, bind and enjoy!

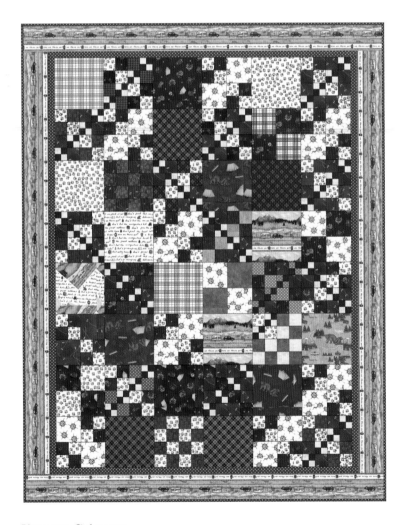

Alternate Colorway

Quilt Layout

VARIATION:
Summer's Meadow

Have you ever seen a meadow so full of wildflowers that you could hardly glimpse the green of the grass? That's what this variation of *MOTHER OF PEARL* (page 26) brings to mind for me. Sometimes nothing can evoke the image of an overgrown meadow in the full bloom of summer more than a softly blended quilt.

Quilt Size: 92" × 116" (Queen)

Block Size: 6" × 6"

Fabric: *Nature's Notebook* by Moda

Pieced by the author, quilted by Bobbi Lang.

This Quilt's Pre-Cuts...

layer cake • jelly roll • charm squares

MATERIALS

FOR PRE-CUTS QUILT

1 layer cake (Blocks)

1 jelly roll (Blocks)

42 pairs of identical 5" charm squares, for a total of 84 squares (Blocks)

Additional yardage

FOR FAT QUARTER QUILT

1 fat quarter bundle or at least 42 coordinating fat quarters (Blocks)

Additional yardage

ADDITIONAL YARDAGE

⅝ yd. small blue print fabric (Flange)

¾ yd. blue and yellow print fabric (Inner Border)

2⅞ yds. large white print fabric cut lengthwise, or 2½ yds. cut crosswise (Outer Border)

⅞ yd. blue fabric (Binding)

BATTING AND BACKING YARDAGE

King size batting (pieced from width to lengthen)

Backing (choose one):

42" wide fabric: 8 yds.
90" wide fabric: 5⅓ yds.
108" wide fabric: 3⅓ yds.

CUTTING INSTRUCTIONS

For Fat Quarter Quilt Only

Using the Fat Quarter Cutting Diagram as a guide, cut from each fat quarter:

(3) 2½" wide jelly roll strips.

(1) 10" wide layer cake strip; subcut 1 pile of 10" squares. Cut the remainder of the 10" strip into (2) 5" charm square strips; subcut into 4 sets of 5" squares.

Follow the instructions below for cutting additional yardage.

For Pre-Cuts and Fat Quarter Quilts

For the Flange, cut (8) 2" strips from the small blue print fabric.

For the Inner Border, cut (9) 2½" strips from the blue and yellow print fabric.

For the Outer Border, cut (4) 8" lengthwise strips from 2⅞ yards of the large white print fabric, or cut (10) 8" crosswise strips from the 2½ yards of the large white print fabric.

Cut 2½" strips from the binding fabric.

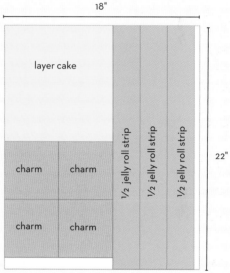

Fat Quarter Cutting Diagram

Sew You Know . . .

If you use pre-cuts, you should have twelve extra 6" blocks. These would make beautiful coordinating pillows for your bed. If you use fat quarters, you will probably have enough extra blocks to make a baby quilt.

Note: The following instructions use 42" long jelly roll strips. If you used fat quarters, double the number of strips in the instructions. For example, ten jelly roll strips equal twenty fat quarter strips.

SEWING INSTRUCTIONS

Off-Side Four Patches (Make 21)

1. Match two identical charm squares. Choose two coordinating pairs for each Four Patch.

2. Sew each square to its coordinate and press the seams toward the darker fabric.

3. Turn one pair upside down and join it to its partner to make the Four Patch block. Press. (Figure 1)

4. Very carefully, trim $2\frac{1}{2}$" off two sides of each Four Patch. You will use the $2\frac{1}{2}$" strips and squares, so set them aside. (Figure 2)

5. With the small square in the upper left-hand corner, trim the right side and bottom of the block so it is exactly $6\frac{1}{2}$" square. (Figure 3)

6. Trim all the $2\frac{1}{2}$" strips from step 4 down to $6\frac{1}{2}$" long. (Figure 4)

Nine Patches (Make 67)

You will need twenty-three dark strips and nineteen light strips.

1. Sew eighteen dark strips to each side of nine light strips. Press. (Figure 5)

2. Sew the remaining ten light strips to each side of the remaining five dark strips. Press. (Figure 6)

3. Crosscut the strips from steps 1 and 2 into $2\frac{1}{2}$" units.

4. To make the Nine Patch blocks, sew a dark-light-dark unit to each side of light-dark-light units. Press. Repeat this step to make sixty-seven blocks. (Figure 7)

5. Set all remaining $2\frac{1}{2}$" × $6\frac{1}{2}$" units aside.

Zigzag Blocks (Make 18)

1. Retrieve eighteen light-dark-light units from the Nine Patch leftovers and eighteen like pairs of pieced rectangles left over from the off-side Four Patches.

2. Join three strips as shown to make the Zigzag blocks. Press. (Figure 8)

Figure 1

Figure 2

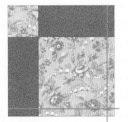

Figure 3

Figure 4

Figure 5

Figure 6

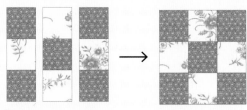

Figure 7

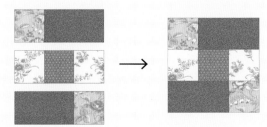

Figure 8

Plain Blocks (Make 42)

Very carefully, trim 3½" off two sides of each layer cake. You will use the 3½" strips and squares, so set them aside. (Figure 9)

Log Blocks (Make 42)

Randomly sew together two coordinating 3½" × 6½" strips from the trimmed layer cakes. Press toward the darker fabric. (Figure 10)

Four Patches (Make 10)

Randomly sew together two 3½" squares from the trimmed layer cakes. Join each pair of squares to another pair to make Four Patch blocks. (Figure 11)

Nine Patches, Take 2 (Make 4)

1. Join all the remaining 2½" squares into columns of three. Add in any leftover strips from the previous Nine Patches you may have.

2. Join three columns to make the Nine Patch blocks. (Figure 12)

ASSEMBLING THE TOP

1. Using the Quilt Layout (page 32) as a guide, lay out the quilt twelve blocks across by sixteen blocks down.

2. Sew the blocks together into rows. Press the seams on odd-numbered rows to one side and even-numbered rows to the other side.

3. Sew the rows together to finish the inner top. Press the seams in one direction.

ADDING THE BORDERS

Border Flange

1. Measure the quilt from top to bottom in several places and average the results. Piece and cut two 2" flange strips to that length.

2. With wrong sides together, fold each strip in half lengthwise and press. Baste one strip to each side of the quilt, matching raw edges. (Figure 13)

3. Measure the quilt from side to side in several places and average the results. Piece and cut two 2" flange strips to that length.

4. Repeat step 2 to baste the flanges to the top and bottom of the quilt.

Inner Border

1. Measure the quilt from top to bottom in several places and average the results. Piece and cut two blue and yellow print border strips that length. Sew one strip to each side of the quilt. Press the seams toward this border.

2. Measure the quilt again from side to side in several places and average the results. Piece and cut the remaining two border strips that length. Sew these strips to the top and bottom of the quilt. Press the seams toward this border.

Outer Border

Repeat the Inner Border steps with the 8" white print strips.

Layer and quilt, bind and enjoy!

Figure 9

Figure 10

Figure 11

Figure 12

Figure 13

Burgoyne in Bloom

The classic Burgoyne Surrounded block evokes images of 18th-century fabrics—a little old and dusty! Well, Burgoyne is finally getting a life! I changed the traditional block a little by trading the middle section with the traditional Window Pane block. Look through Burgoyne's window at the colors of spring—full of new life!

Quilt Size: $68\frac{1}{2}$" × 88" (Twin)

Block Size: $19\frac{1}{2}$" × $19\frac{1}{2}$"

Pieced by the author, quilted by Bobbi Lang.

Choosing Fabrics

I used the *Spring Magic* and *Bella Solids* Moda pre-cut lines for this quilt. If they are not available, choose pre-cuts that feature solids and densely printed, saturated pastels. Focus on greens, pinks and yellows. Purchase additional yardage as specified in a background color that coordinates with your particular pre-cut line.

- - - - - - - - - - - - - - - -

This Quilt's Pre-Cuts...

charm squares • honey bun

MATERIALS

FOR PRE-CUTS QUILT

At least 24 floral 5" charm squares (Window Pane Blocks)

48 solid 5" charm squares (Corner Blocks)

1 honey bun (Side Strip Rectangular Blocks and Nine Patch Blocks)

Additional yardage

FOR FAT QUARTER QUILT

1 floral fat quarter bundle, or at least 12 floral fat quarters and 4 solid fat quarters

Additional yardage

ADDITIONAL YARDAGE

4¼ yds. white fabric (Blocks and Wide Border)

⅓ yd. light green fabric (Narrow Border)

1¼ yds. small print fabric (Binding)

BATTING AND BACKING YARDAGE

Double/full size batting

Backing (choose one):

42" wide fabric: 5⅛ yds.
90" wide fabric: 2⅝ yds.
108" wide fabric: 2⅛ yds.

CUTTING INSTRUCTIONS

For Fat Quarter Quilt Only

Using the Fat Quarter Floral Prints Cutting Diagram as a guide, cut from each floral fat quarter:

(8) 1½" honey bun strips.

(1) 5" charm square strip; subcut it into 5" charm squares.

Using the Fat Quarter Solids Cutting Diagram as a guide, cut from each solid fat quarter:

(3) 5" charm square strips; subcut into 5" squares.

Follow the instructions below for subcutting pre-cuts and cutting additional yardage.

For Pre-Cuts and Fat Quarter Quilts

Cut 48 solid charm squares in half; subcut them into 2½" x 3½" rectangles for the Corner blocks.

Cut 2 honey bun strips (or 4 fat quarter strips) into (48) 1½" squares for the Side Strip Rectangular blocks.

From the white fabric:

For the Window Pane blocks, cut (3) 5" strips; subcut them into (24) 5" squares. Cut (3) 2" strips; subcut them into 2" × 4½" rectangles. Cut 3 more 2" strips; subcut them into 2" × 10" rectangles.

For the Side Strip Rectangular blocks, cut (14) 1½" strips; subcut 2 of them into (48) 1½" squares. Cut (12) 3½" strips; subcut them into (48) 3½" × 10" rectangles.

For the Nine Patch blocks, cut (8) 1½" strips.

For the Four Patch blocks, cut (4) 1½" strips.

For the Wide Border, cut (8) 4" strips.

Cut (7) 1½" strips from the light green fabric for the Narrow Border.

Cut 2½" strips from the binding fabric.

Fat Quarter Floral Prints Cutting Diagram

Fat Quarter Solids Cutting Diagram

Note: The following instructions use 42" long honey bun strips. If you used fat quarters, double the number of strips. For example, ten honey bun strips equal twenty fat quarter strips.

SEWING INSTRUCTIONS

Nine Patch Blocks (Make 48)

You will need ten honey bun strips and eight white strips.

1. Sew eight floral honey bun strips to each side of four white strips. (Note: White fabric is shown in pink throughout illustrations for contrast.) Press away from the white. (Figure 1)

2. Sew the remaining four white strips to each side of the remaining two floral honey bun strips. Press away from the white. (Figure 2)

3. Crosscut the strips from steps 1 and 2 into 1½" units. (Figure 3)

4. To make Nine Patch blocks, sew a floral-white-floral unit to each side of the white-floral-white units. Press. Trim to 3½" square. Repeat this step to make forty-eight blocks. (Figure 4)

Four Patch Blocks (Make 48)

You will need four honey bun strips and four white strips.

1. Sew each white strip to a floral honey bun strip. Press away from the white. (Figure 5)

2. Crosscut each strip into twenty-eight 1½" units. (Figure 6)

3. For each of the forty-eight Four Patches, turn one unit upside down and sew it to another. Press. Trim to 2½" square. (Figure 7)

Figure 1

Figure 2

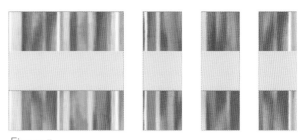

Figure 3

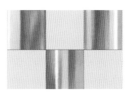

Figure 4

Figure 5

Figure 6

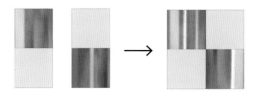

Figure 7

Window Pane Blocks (Make 12)

1. Choose twelve identical pairs of 5" floral charm squares (for a total of twenty-four squares). Draw a diagonal line from corner to corner on the back of them. (Figure 8)

2. Pair up each of those charm squares with a white 5" square, right sides together. (Figure 9)

3. Sew on either side of the drawn line with a ¼" seam allowance. (Figure 10)

4. Cut along the drawn line. Press. (Figure 11)

5. Open up each triangle and press the seam allowances toward the print side. Trim the blocks to 4½" square, being careful to keep the seams in the corners. You will have forty-eight blocks. (Figure 12)

6. For each block, choose two 2" × 4½" strips and one 2" × 10" strip. Lay the triangle squares out with the strips and sew them together, row by row. Press toward the strips. Trim the blocks to 10" square. (Figure 13)

Side Strip Blocks (Make 48)

1. For each of these rectangular blocks, you will need a honey bun strip, a 1½" honey bun square, a 3½" × 10" white strip, a 1½" white strip and a 1½" white square. (Figure 14)

2. Sew the 1½" white strip to the honey bun strip. Crosscut into eight 4¾" lengths. Press toward the honey bun strip.

3. Sew a 1½" white square to a 1½" honey bun square. Press away from the white.

4. Turn the honey bun square strip upside down. Sew the 4¾" strips to both sides of it.

5. Lay the rectangle out and sew the 3½" white strip to the honey bun edge of the step 4 unit. Press away from the white. Trim to 5½"× 10".

Figure 8   Figure 9

Figure 10   Figure 11

Figure 12

Figure 13

Figure 14

Corner Blocks (Make 48)

1. For each of these Corner blocks, you will need two solid 2½" x 3½" rectangles, a Nine Patch block and a Four Patch block.

2. Lay out the units and sew them together in rows. Press. Trim to 5½" square. (Figure 15)

Burgoyne Blocks (Make 12)

1. For each Burgoyne block, you will need one Window Pane block, four Side Strip blocks and four Corner blocks.

2. Lay out the units, watching the orientation very carefully. Sew them together row by row. Press. Trim to 20" square. (Figure 16)

ASSEMBLING THE QUILT TOP

1. Lay out the blocks according to the Quilt Layout (page 41), three blocks across by four rows down.

2. Sew each row of blocks together. Press the even rows one way and the odd rows the other way.

3. Sew the rows together to complete the inner quilt top. Press.

ADDING THE BORDERS

Border 1 (Green)

1. Measure the quilt from top to bottom in several places and average the results. Piece together and cut two of the 1½" green border strips that length. Sew those strips to the sides of the quilt. Press toward this border.

2. Measure the quilt again from side to side in several places and average the results. Piece together and cut two more 1½" strips that length. Sew those strips to the top and bottom of the quilt. Press toward this border.

Border 2 (White)

In the same manner as you used for Border 1, measure and sew the 4" white borders to complete the quilt top.

Layer and quilt, bind and enjoy!

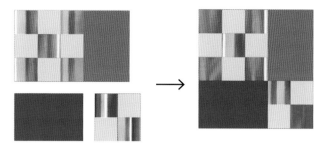

Figure 15

Figure 16

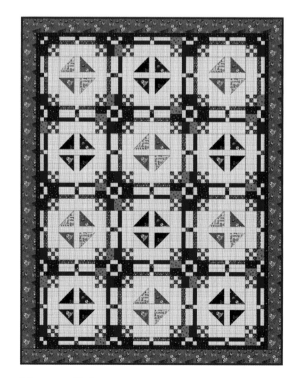

Alternate Colorway

Quilt Layout

Great Bouncing Begonias

This is a simple but lively pieced and appliquéd quilt. The tossed begonias emulate the way your eye travels around the pieced blocks. You will learn how to use fabric you "make" to add visual interest to the appliquéd begonias.

Quilt Size: 73" × 87½"
(Double/Full)

Block Size: 13" × 13"

Pieced and quilted by the author.

Choosing Fabrics

I used the *Make Life* Moda pre-cut line for this quilt. Try choosing pre-cuts that feature muted colors with a focus on olive green, browns and Turkey red. Or use any line that has a spectrum of contrasting colors. Purchase additional yardage as specified in colors that coordinate with your particular pre-cut line.

- -

This Quilt's Pre-Cuts...

jelly roll • charm squares

MATERIALS

FOR PRE-CUTS QUILT

1 jelly roll (Blocks and Appliqués)

32 pairs of identical 5" charm squares, for a total of 64 charm squares (Four Patches)

Additional yardage

FOR FAT QUARTER QUILT

1 fat quarter bundle or at least 20 coordinating fat quarters (Blocks, Appliqués and Optional Scrappy Binding)

Additional yardage

ADDITIONAL YARDAGE

1 yd. background fabric (Appliqué Background)

$^2/_3$ yd. coordinating fabric 1 (Inner Border)

$2^1/_4$ yds. coordinating fabric 2 (Outer Border)

$^3/_4$ yd. coordinating fabric 3 (Binding)

BATTING AND BACKING YARDAGE

Double/full size batting

Backing (choose one):

42" wide fabric: $5^1/_8$ yds.
90" wide fabric: $2^5/_8$ yds.
108" wide fabric: $2^1/_4$ yds.

EXTRA MATERIALS

Templates (page 122)

Template plastic

Fusible web

Fine pencil or chalk

CUTTING INSTRUCTIONS

For Fat Quarter Quilt Only

Using the Fat Quarter Cutting Diagram as a guide, cut from each fat quarter:

(4) $2^1/_2$" wide jelly roll strips for Blocks and Optional Scrappy Binding.

(1) 5" wide charm square strip; subcut into 5" squares.

Follow the instructions below for cutting additional yardage.

For Pre-Cut and Fat Quarter Quilts

From the appliqué background fabric, cut (2) 14" strips; subcut to (2) 14" × 30" panel pieces.

From the Inner Border fabric, cut (9) $2^1/_2$" strips; subcut 2 of the strips in half to equal approximately $2^1/_2$" × 21".

From the Outer Border fabric, cut (4) $8^1/_2$" wide × length of fabric (LoF) strips.

From the binding fabric, cut $2^1/_2$" bias strips.

Fat Quarter Cutting Diagram

SEWING INSTRUCTIONS

Four Patch Blocks (Make 16)

1. Pair up each charm with its matching charm. (Figure 1)

2. From the paired charms, pair up sets of charms. (Figure 2)

3. Sew each charm to its coordinating charm. Press seams toward the darker block. (Figure 3)

4. Turn one pair of charms upside down and sew it to its coordinating pair to make a Four Patch. Press. Repeat to make sixteen Four Patches. (Figure 4)

5. Trim the Four Patch blocks to measure exactly 9½" square.

6. Lay the blocks out on a design board, four across and four down. Rearrange them freely until you are pleased with the balance of colors and prints.

7. To maintain the arrangement, label each block using a small piece of paper and a pin. Place the label in the upper left quadrant of each Four Patch. This way you will not lose your favorite block orientation while you are cutting the frames. (Figure 5)

Frame the Blocks

1. Remove the large prints from the jelly roll and remaining charm squares and set them aside. The solids, tone-on-tones and small prints are what you will use for this step.

2. For the corner squares, match up one of these charm squares or ¼ (10") of a jelly roll strip to each Four Patch block. (Figure 6)

3. To choose your framing strips, match up one of the remaining large-print whole jelly roll strips to each Four Patch block. (Figure 7)

4. Stack each Four Patch block's frame and corner block fabric onto the block. (Figure 8) Stack the blocks up and carry them over to your cutting table.

Figure 1

Figure 2

Figure 3

Figure 4

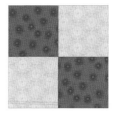

Figure 5

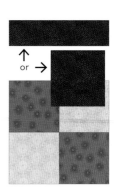

Figure 6

Figure 7

Figure 8

Sew You Know . . .

Depending on your fabrics, you have many options here. You may pair a dark pair with a light pair, a solid pair with a print pair, even a warm pair (yellow, orange and red) with a cool pair (green, blue and purple). The choices are up to you!

5. From the charm square or partial jelly roll strip, cut four 2½" corner squares for each block. Stack them back onto the block. (Figure 9)

6. From the jelly roll strip, cut four 9½" strips for each frame. Stack them back onto the block. (Figure 10)

7. Sew a 9½" strip to two opposite sides of its Four Patch block. Press toward the strip. (Figure 11)

8. Sew one 2½" square to each end of the remaining two strips for each block. Press toward the strip. (Figure 12)

9. Sew these strips to the top and bottom of each block. Press toward the strip. (Figure 13)

10. Trim the finished blocks to exactly 13½" square

Appliquéing the Panel

1. With right sides together, sew the two panel pieces together along the short ends. Press.

2. Following the Make Fabric instructions (page 7), make a 12" × 21" light fabric and a 16" × 21" dark fabric.

3. If you are going to fuse the appliqués, adhere the fusible webbing onto the back of these fabrics according to the manufacturer's directions.

4. Trace four 6" begonias and eight 4½" begonias onto the fusible web, using the 6" and 4½" begonia templates. Cut out the begonias.

5. Fuse webbing onto the backs of scraps for the twelve flower dots.

6. Trace the flower dots onto the scraps, using the 2½" template. Cut out the dots.

7. Using Figure 14 as a guide or your own creative design, arrange the appliqué pieces within a 10" × 48" area of the panel.

8. Fuse and appliqué the motifs onto the panel when you are pleased with the arrangement.

Note: I used a blanket stitch to appliqué the motifs. My settings were 3.0mm wide and 2.5mm long.

9. Trim the panel to 13" × 52½".

Figure 9

Figure 10

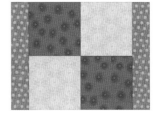

Figure 12

Figure 11

Figure 13

Figure 14

ASSEMBLING THE PIECED BLOCKS

1. Arrange the framed blocks into four rows of four blocks each, referring to the arrangement you chose earlier.

2. Sew the blocks into rows. Press seams to one side on odd-numbered rows and to the other side on even-numbered rows. Sew the rows together. Press.

ADDING THE BORDERS

Inner Border (Red)

1. Sew one cut border piece to a whole strip. Trim the strip to 52½" long.

2. Sew this border strip to the bottom of the appliqué panel. Press toward the strip.

3. Sew the appliqué/border panel to the top edge of the quilt with the border strip next to the pieced blocks. Press toward the strip.

4. Sew two long border strips together end-to-end to make each of the side borders.

5. Measure the quilt from top to bottom in several places. Average the lengths and cut the two strips that length.

6. Sew one strip to each side of the top. Press toward the strips.

7. Sew each remaining cut border piece to a whole strip.

8. Measure your quilt from side to side in several places. Average that length and cut these two remaining border strips that length.

9. Sew one strip to the top and the other to the bottom of the quilt. Press toward this border. (Figure 15)

Outer Border (Olive)

Using the 8½" wide strips of fabric, follow steps 5, 6, 8 and 9 for the Inner Border to sew the Outer Border.

Scalloped Edge

1. Trace the enlarged scalloped edge template onto a piece of template plastic and cut it out.

2. Lining up the template with each of the four corners of the quilt, draw the scalloped edge directly onto your quilt top with a fine pencil or chalk. This drawn line will be your cutting line.

3. Sandwich and quilt your quilt, choosing a pattern that fits at least ½" inside the markings for the scalloped edge.

4. Square up the quilt, retracing the corners if necessary. Trim the scalloped edge through all the layers.

Bind your quilt and cuddle up!

Figure 15

Alternate Colorway

Quilt Layout

VARIATION:
Jelly Roll Charm

Jelly rolls and charm squares are so wonderfully compatible. The potential variations are probably endless. This variation of GREAT BOUNCING BEGONIAS (page 42) eliminates the appliqué panel. I got a little "scrappy" with the charm squares, and I used white for alternate squares in the Four Patch blocks—white really helps those bright colors pop!

Quilt Size: 73" × 73" (Double/Full)

Block Size: 13" × 13"

Fabric: Love U by Moda

Pieced by April Greenway-Horsman and author, quilted by Bobbi Lang.

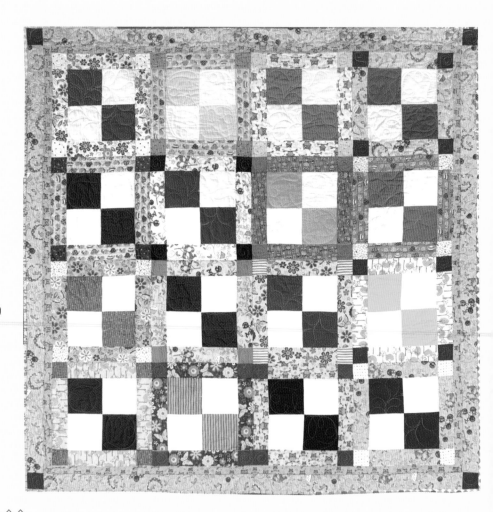

This Quilt's Pre-Cuts...

jelly roll • charm squares

MATERIALS

FOR PRE-CUTS QUILT

1 jelly roll (Blocks)

16 pairs of identical 5" charm squares, for a total of 32 charm squares (Four Patches)

Additional yardage

FOR FAT QUARTER QUILT

1 fat quarter bundle or at least 8 coordinating fat quarters (Blocks)

Additional yardage

ADDITIONAL YARDAGE

$2/3$ yd. white fabric (Blocks)

$1/2$ yd. coordinating fabric 1 (Inner Border)

$2\frac{1}{8}$ yds. coordinating fabric 2 (Outer Border)

$5/8$ yd. coordinating fabric 3 (Binding)

BATTING AND BACKING YARDAGE

Double/full size batting

Backing (choose one):

42" wide fabric: $4\frac{3}{8}$ yds.
90" wide fabric: $2\frac{1}{4}$ yds.
108" wide fabric: $2\frac{1}{4}$ yds.

CUTTING INSTRUCTIONS

For Fat Quarter Quilt Only

Using the Fat Quarter Cutting Diagram as a guide, cut from each fat quarter:

(4) $2\frac{1}{2}$" wide jelly roll strips.

(1) 5" wide charm square strip; subcut into 5" squares.

Follow the instructions below for cutting additional yardage.

For Pre-Cuts and Fat Quarter Quilts

From the Inner Border fabric, cut (6) $2\frac{1}{2}$" strips; subcut 2 of the strips in half to equal approximately $2\frac{1}{2}$" × 21".

From the Outer Border fabric, cut (4) $8\frac{1}{2}$" wide × length of fabric (LOF) strips.

From the binding fabric, cut $2\frac{1}{2}$" strips.

Fat Quarter Cutting Diagram

SEWING INSTRUCTIONS

Follow the Sewing Instructions for *GREAT BOUNCING BEGONIAS* (page 42), skipping the "Appliquéing the Panel" section.

ADDING THE BORDERS

Inner Border

1. Measure the quilt from top to bottom in several places and average the results. Piece together and cut two of the $2\frac{1}{2}$" border strips that length. Sew one strip to each side of the quilt. Press the seams toward this border.

2. Measure the quilt again from side to side in several places and average the results. Cut two more strips that length. Sew these strips to the top and bottom of the quilt. Press the seams toward this border.

Outer Border

Using the $8\frac{1}{2}$" wide strips of fabric, follow the instructions for the Inner Border, except you will not need to piece the lengthwise cuts of fabric.

Quilt, bind and cuddle up!

Hollyhocks

This collection of hollyhocks is a tribute to my dad's green thumb. He would plant hollyhocks wherever he lived, and all he had to do was touch them to make them produce gorgeous, giant blossoms! For me, making this quilt is a lot easier. *HOLLYHOCKS* is an art quilt, so enjoy some freedom with it!

Quilt Size: 33" × 70"
(Wall Hanging)

Pieced and quilted by the author.

Choosing Fabrics

I used Robert Kaufman's *Kona Cotton Pastels* and Moda's *Bella Solids* for this quilt. They are consistently available, but you may choose any pre-cuts that read as solids, like tone-on-tones or certain batiks. Purchase additional yardage as specified in colors that coordinate with your particular pre-cut line.

- -

This Quilt's Pre-Cuts...

jelly roll • charm squares

MATERIALS

FOR PRE-CUTS QUILT

1 jelly roll of pastel solids (Sunrise Stratum and Pieced Border)

3 charm square packs of pastel solids (Blossoms and Leaves)

Additional yardage

FOR FAT QUARTER QUILT

1 fat quarter bundle or at least 16 solid pastel fat quarters (Sunrise Stratum, Pieced Border, Blossoms and Leaves)

Additional yardage

ADDITIONAL YARDAGE

1½ yds. bright green fabric (Stalks and Inner Border)

¾ yd. light green fabric (Binding)

BATTING AND BACKING YARDAGE

Twin size batting (pieced from width to lengthen)

Backing (choose one):

    42" wide fabric: 2⅛ yds.
    90" wide fabric: 1⅛ yds.
    108" wide fabric: 1⅛ yds.

EXTRA SUPPLIES

Appliqué templates (found on pages 122–123)

Plastic or Mylar template material

Fusible web

Quilters' or dressmakers' chalk

CUTTING INSTRUCTIONS

For Fat Quarter Quilt Only

Using the Fat Quarter Cutting Diagram as a guide, cut from each fat quarter:

    (5) 2½" wide jelly roll strips.

    (4) 5" square charm squares.

From the binding fabric, cut 2½" bias strips.

Fat Quarter Cutting Diagram

MAKING THE SUNRISE STRATUM

1. Cut all the jelly roll strips in half to about 21" long. Lay out the strips to create a subtly shifting stratum of sunrise colors using the Quilt Layout (page 57) as a guideline. Use secondary tones (peach, violet and green) to blend between primary tones (yellow, pink and blue). Use forty to forty-five total strips in the stratum.

2. Cut most of the strips lengthwise at any angle that goes the entire length of the strip; do not leave less than $3/4$" on either end. Balance out how much of the strip is cut from the left end with another cut about the same amount from the right end so the background does not skew sideways. (Figure 1)

3. When you are satisfied with the layout, sew the strips together. Only sew a few together at once, making sure the sides are not too skewed before sewing the next group of strips. Press all seams open to reduce bulk.

4. Square up the finished stratum. Trim both sides straight and even with the end of the innermost strip on both sides. The resulting length will depend on how many strips you used in your stratum. The width should measure approximately 20"–21" wide. (Figure 2)

Sew You Know . . .

When looking at the natural sky, the darkest blues are at the zenith, so place the darkest blues at the top of the stratum. Then gently lighten the sky as you proceed down, integrating various blues and blue-violets. Toward the middle of the stratum, introduce the bright sunrise colors, shifting from red-violets to pinks and peaches, then yellows and finally orange. Now you are on terra firma and can incorporate more blue-violets for mountain ranges, blues for water and, last but not least, greens for grass.

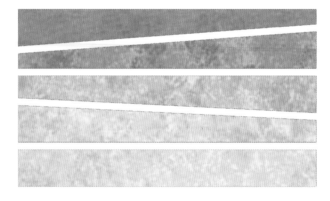

Figure 1

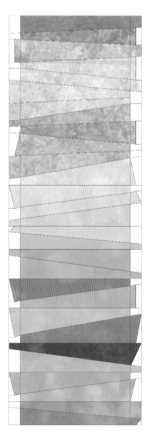

Figure 2

MAKING THE HOLLYHOCK STALKS

1. Cut off ½ yard of the bright green fabric and set it aside for the Inner Border. Remove the selvages from the remaining yard and cut it in half into two 18" pieces. With right sides together, stitch two short ends together to result in a double-width piece of fabric.

2. Draw three stalks onto the paper side of fusible web as follows:

   a. Left stalk: 25" tall, 2" wide at the bottom, tapering to 1" wide at the top

   b. Center stalk: 48" tall, 3" wide at the bottom, tapering to 1" wide at the top

   c. Right stalk: 35" tall, 2½" wide at the bottom, tapering to ½" wide at the top

3. Cut them out, leaving at least ¼" extra web on all sides. Fuse the web onto the back of the green fabric according to the manufacturer's instructions. Cut out the stalks on the drawn lines.

4. To orient the stalks on the background stratum, draw three lines with chalk. Starting at the bottom edge of the stratum, make marks 5", 11¾" and 15¾" in from the left side.

5. Using a long ruler or yardstick, extend the first mark 25" straight up the length of the quilt. Extend the middle mark up 48" and the final mark up 35". (Figure 3)

6. Line up the right side of the shortest stalk with the 25" chalk line, the right side of the tallest stalk with the 48" chalk line and the left side of the remaining stalk with the 35" chalk line. Fuse in place. Appliqué stitch the sides of all three stalks. (Figure 4)

ADDING THE GREEN INNER BORDER

1. Cut six 3" strips from the bright green border fabric. Sew two of the strips together end-to-end resulting in a strip about 84" long. Repeat to make a second 84" long strip.

2. Measure the quilt lengthwise several times through the middle and average the results. Cut the two long strips to that length. Sew them to each side of the quilt top. Press the seams toward the border.

3. Measure the quilt several times across the width. Average the results and cut the remaining two strips that length. Sew them to the top and bottom of the quilt top. Press the seams toward the border. (Figure 4)

4. This border needs to measure a multiple of 2, plus ½" for seam allowances. (For instance, the quilt in the photo measured 24½" wide at this point; 24 is a multiple of 2, plus you have ½" for the two seam allowances.) Measure the quilt carefully and trim the borders accordingly.

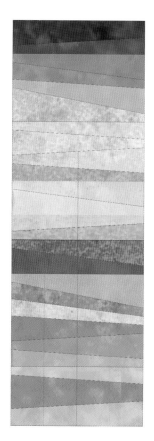

Draw three reference lines.
→

Figure 3

Figure 4

ADDING THE LEAF AND BLOSSOM APPLIQUÉS

1. Trace and cut out the leaf and blossom appliqué templates from template material. Use both sides of the templates to add variety to the shapes of the leaves and blossoms.

2. Fuse all the charm squares onto fusible web. Cut the charm squares apart and sort into three piles: greens for leaves, yellows for flower centers, and other colors for blossoms.

3. Trace the three leaf templates onto the green charm squares. (You can get two small leaves from each charm square and, if you're careful, a small and medium leaf.) Cut out as many leaves as you can.

4. Trace the embroidery veins onto the leaves with a fine pencil.

5. Trace the round and oval flower center templates onto about five yellow charm squares, fitting as many as you can on each square. Put the rest of the yellow charm squares in the pile of blossom charm squares. Cut out the flower centers.

6. From the rest of the charm squares, trace the three sizes of flower blossoms. Fit as many as you can on each charm square. Cut out the blossoms.

ASSEMBLING THE APPLIQUÉS

1. Using the Quilt Layout as a guide, place the appliqués onto the background. I've listed a few rules of thumb here, but the quilt is the artwork and should have its own unique personality:

   - The leaves and flowers are denser and larger at the bottom, and thin out and get smaller as they move up the quilt.

   - Flowers may be layered one, two or three blossoms deep. Layering the blossoms off center makes them look like they're facing a certain direction. If you place most of them facing inward and upward, the eye travels up the length of the quilt. Don't be too consistent though!

   - All the edges need to overlap each other in totally haphazard ways. You can observe this in the photo below. This creates a three-dimensional effect.

   - Place flowers and leaves overlapping the border toward the bottom and sides of the quilt. This moves the eye outward and helps incorporate the borders into the overall picture.

   - You probably have more appliqués than you need. This just gives you more options. You do not have to use all of them.

2. Once you have come up with a pleasing arrangement, fuse the appliqués in place.

3. Using a dark thread for contrast, straight stitch about ⅛" in from the edge of every appliqué piece. At the same time, embroider the veins on the leaves.

Photo provided by author.

ADDING THE PIECED BORDER

Corner Blocks (Make 4)

1. Cut a 6½" piece off of twenty-four leftover jelly roll strips of various colors.

2. Sew three of the strips together side by side, and then trim to a 6" square. Repeat to make eight blocks. (Figure 5)

3. Draw a diagonal line with a pencil or chalk on the back of four of the blocks. (Figure 6)

4. Pair up each block that has a drawn line with a block without a line. Place the blocks right sides together with the seams in both blocks running the same direction. With the chalk-marked block on top, stitch on the line from corner to corner. Trim off the excess fabric on one side of the line, leaving a ¼" seam allowance. (Figure 7)

5. Open up the blocks and press. (Figure 8)

Piano Keys

1. Cut the remaining jelly roll strips into 5" lengths.

2. Divide the length of the quilt without seam allowances by 2 to get the number of strips you need.

For example, if the quilt has a 62½" border length, 62 divided by 2 is 31, so it needs thirty-one strips in the side border. If the top and bottom borders are 24½" wide, there are twelve strips in those borders.

3. Arrange the strips around the quilt, mixing up all the colors. Sew the strips for each side border together. Press. Sew them to the sides of the quilt. Press toward the green border. (Figure 9)

Figure 5   Figure 6

Figure 7   Figure 8

Figure 9 (Appliqués omitted for clarity)

4. Sew the strips for the top and bottom borders together, and sew a corner block to each end. Press. Be sure that the diagonal seams point to the inside of the quilt. (Figure 10)

5. Sew the borders to the top and bottom of the quilt. Press toward the green border. The outer edges of the corner blocks will stick out past the edges of the quilt. (Figure 11)

SHAPING THE QUILT EDGE

1. Trace and cut out the quilt edge templates from a piece of template plastic.

2. Starting at one of the corners of the quilt, trace the edge of the templates as close to the outer edge of the quilt as you can. Repeat drawing the curves until you get to within one curve of the center of the edge. Repeat this process on all four sides.

3. If the curves do not meet perfectly in the center, and they probably will not, create a gentle curve to fill the gap. You can use part of the edge of any round object like a cup or a plate to make this gentle curve.

4. This is the cutting line for the edge of the quilt. Do not cut it yet.

FINISHING THE QUILT

1. Sandwich and quilt the quilt, choosing a pattern that fits at least 1/2" inside the markings for the curved edges.

2. Square up the quilt, retracing the edges if you need to. Trim the curved edges through all the layers.

3. Cut the binding on the bias for these curved edges.

4. Bind the piece of art and enjoy!

Top

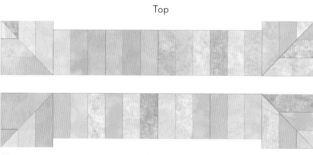

Figure 10

Bottom

Alternate Colorway

Figure 11

Quilt Layout

Mixed Fruit Sorbet

I remember thinking that sorbet was just glorified (and expensive) sherbet. And then I tasted it. Sherbet is good, but sorbet is . . . *wow*! When I was designing this quilt, I was thinking of sherbet, but when it was done, I saw *wow*—sorbet! Chain piecing makes sewing these teensy checkers a snap. Trim up the charm squares, throw in a jelly roll, and don't mix too well! Fruit sorbets are always better when they are a little chunky!

Quilt Size: 65" × 73" (Throw)

Block Size: 8" × 8"

Pieced by the author, quilted by Bobbi Lang.

Choosing Fabrics

I used Moda's *Bella Solids* in pastels in conjunction with a Hoffman *Sherbet* Bali Pop for this quilt. They are consistently available, but you may also choose pre-cuts that feature bright crayon colors. Focus on greens, purples and navy. Or use any solid line in a spectrum of contrasting colors that would complement your prints. Purchase additional yardage as specified in colors that coordinate with your particular pre-cut line.

- -

This Quilt's Pre-Cuts...

jelly roll • charm squares

MATERIALS

FOR PRE-CUTS QUILT

1 batik jelly roll (Blocks and Borders 2 and 4)

(84) 5" solid charm squares (Blocks)

Additional yardage

FOR FAT EIGHTH QUILT

1 batik fat eighth bundle or at least 28 batik fat eighths

1 solid fat eighth bundle or at least 12 solid fat eighths

Additional yardage

ADDITIONAL YARDAGE

1¼ yds. white fabric (Blocks and Border 3)

1¼ yds. navy blue fabric (Blocks, Border 1 and Binding)

BATTING AND BACKING YARDAGE

Twin size batting

Backing (choose one):

42" wide fabric: 4 yds.

90" wide fabric: 2 yds.

108" wide fabric: 2 yds.

CUTTING INSTRUCTIONS

For Fat Eighth Quilt Only

Using the Fat Eighth Cutting Diagram as a guide, cut:

(3) 2½" jelly roll strips from each batik fat eighth (Diagram 1).

(2) 4½" charm square strips from each solid fat eighth; subcut into 4½" squares (Diagram 2).

Follow the instructions below for subcutting pre-cuts and cutting additional yardage.

For Pre-Cuts and Fat Eighth Quilts

Trim each charm square to a 4½" square.

From the jelly roll strips:

Cut 11 jelly roll strips each into 4 equal segments (approximately 11" each).

Cut the remaining jelly roll strips into (74) 2½" squares for Border 2 and (74) 4½" matching strips for Border 4.

Cut 46 more 4½" strips for Border 4.

From the white fabric, cut:

(15) 1½" strips for the Four Patches.

(6) 1½" strips; subcut 4 of them into (11) 10½" strips and (4) 2½" strips for Border 3.

(1) 4½" strip; subcut into (4) 4½" squares for Border 4.

From the navy blue fabric, cut:

(15) 1½" strips for Four Patches.

(6) 1½" strips for Border 1.

(1) 1½" strip; subcut into (8) 2½" lengths for Border 2 corners.

(3) 1½" strips; subcut 1 strip into (11) 2½" pieces for Border 3.

2½" strips for binding.

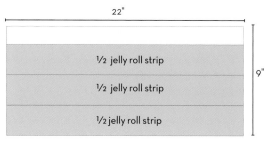

Fat Eighth Batiks Cutting Diagram 1

Fat Eighth Solids Cutting Diagram 2

Sew You Know . . .

If you want to use fat quarters, you may use 14 batiks and 6 solids. Lay the Cutting Diagrams side by side on the fat quarters.

SEWING INSTRUCTIONS

Four Patch Units (Make 202)

You will need fifteen navy blue strips and fifteen white strips.

1. Sew each white strip to a navy blue strip. Press away from the white. (Figure 1)

2. Crosscut each strip into twenty-eight 1½" units. (Figure 2)

3. To make each of the Four Patch units, turn one unit upside down and stitch it to another. Press. Trim the blocks to 2½" square. (Figure 3)

Ten Patch Blocks (Make 42)

You will need 168 of the 2½" Four Patch blocks and forty-four 11" jelly roll strips.

1. With right sides together, place four Four Patch units close together along one edge of each jelly roll strip. Be very careful to place them in the correct orientation: the navy square must be in the lower left and upper right corners. Sew. Press seams toward the jelly roll strips. (Figure 4)

2. Carefully crosscut the units apart into 2½" × 4½" rectangles. (Figure 5)

3. To make each of the Ten Patch blocks, turn one unit upside down and stitch it to another. Press. Trim the blocks to 4½" square. (Figure 6)

Assembling the Block (Make 42)

1. Match up each set of identical Ten Patch blocks with two coordinating 4½" solid squares. (Figure 7)

2. Sew each Ten Patch block to its solid square, once again maintaining the correct orientation as shown in the illustration. (Figure 8)

3. To make each block, turn one unit upside down and stitch it to another, once again maintaining the correct orientation. Press. Trim blocks to 8½" square. (Figure 9)

Figure 1

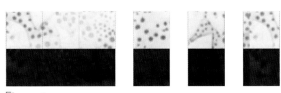

Figure 2

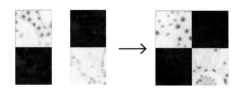

Figure 3

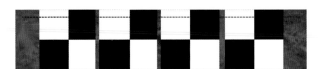

Figure 4

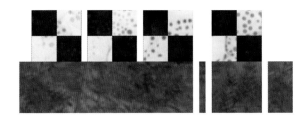

Figure 5

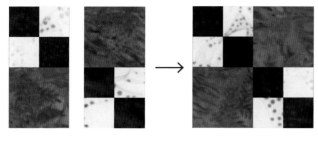

Figure 6

Figure 8

Figure 7

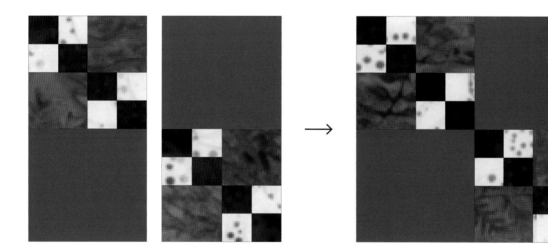

Figure 9

ASSEMBLING THE QUILT TOP

1. Lay out the blocks according to the Quilt Layout (page 63), six blocks across by seven rows down.

2. Sew each row of blocks together. Press seams on the even rows one way and the odd rows the other way.

3. Sew the rows together to complete the inner quilt top. Press.

ADDING THE BORDERS

Border 1 (Navy)

1. Sew together three of the 1½" navy border strips end-to-end. From the resulting strip, cut two 58½" long strips. Sew these strips to the sides of the quilt. Press toward this border.

2. Sew together three of the 1½" navy border strips end-to-end. From the resulting strip, cut two 50½" long strips. Sew these strips to the top and bottom of the quilt. Press toward this border.

Border 2 (Pieced Four Patches)

You will need the remaining 2½" Four Patch units, seventy-four 2½" jelly roll squares, and eight 1½" × 2½" navy strips.

1. Use the Quilt Layout to carefully lay out the Four Patches, squares and navy strips around the quilt edge. Watch the orientation of the Four Patch blocks. Try to match the colors of the jelly roll squares with the colors of the adjacent blocks in the quilt top wherever you can.

   - Side borders layout from top to bottom: navy strip, one Four Patch, six squares, two Four Patches, six squares, two Four Patches, six squares, two Four Patches, two squares, one Four Patch, navy strip

   - Top border layout from left to right: one Four patch, navy strip, one Four Patch, six squares, two Four Patches, six squares, two Four Patches, six squares, one Four Patch, navy strip, one Four Patch

   - Bottom border layout from left to right: one Four Patch, navy strip, one Four Patch, two squares, two Four Patches, six squares, two Four Patches, six squares, two Four Patches, two squares, one Four Patch, navy strip, one Four Patch

2. Sew the side border blocks together and press away from the Four Patches. Sew the borders to the sides of the quilt. Press toward Border 1.

3. Sew the top and bottom border blocks together and press away from the Four Patches. Sew the borders to the top and bottom of the quilt. Press toward Border 1.

Border 3 (Navy and White Pieces)

You will need eleven 1½" × 10½" white pieces, four 1½" × 2½" white pieces, two whole navy and white strips, and eleven 1½" × 2½" navy pieces.

1. Sew each whole navy strip to a whole white strip. Press toward the navy strip.

2. Crosscut the strips into 1½" units.

3. Using the Quilt Layout, carefully lay out these units and other pieces around the quilt edge.

4. Sew the pieces in the side borders together. Press. Sew the borders to the sides of the quilt. Press.

5. Sew the top and bottom border pieces together. Press. Sew the borders to the top and bottom of the quilt. Press.

Border 4 (Jelly Roll Strips)

1. Lay out (120) 4½" jelly roll strips and the four 4½" white squares around the quilt edges, matching colors in Border 2 where you can.

2. Sew the strips in the side borders together. Press. Sew the borders to the sides of the quilt. Press toward this border.

3. Sew the top and bottom border pieces together with the white squares on the ends. Press. Sew the borders to the top and bottom of the quilt. Press toward this border.

Layer and quilt, bind and enjoy!

Alternate Colorway

Quilt Layout

VARIATION:
Hugs 'n' Prayers

In honor of those in my family who have suffered through and triumphed over breast cancer, I made this quilt in pinks and whites. This variation of *MIXED FRUIT SORBET* (page 58) has only one simple border. It memorializes a treasury of hugs and prayers.

Quilt Size: 57" × 73" (Throw)

Block Size: 8" × 8"

Fabric: *Quilt Pink* by Moda

Pieced by the author, quilted by Bobbi Lang.

This Quilt's Pre-Cuts...

jelly roll • charm squares

MATERIALS

FOR PRE-CUTS QUILT

1 jelly roll (Blocks)

48 pairs of identical 5" charm squares, for a total of 96 squares (Blocks)

Additional yardage

FOR FAT QUARTER QUILT

1 fat quarter bundle or at least 24 coordinating fat quarters

Additional yardage

ADDITIONAL YARDAGE

$^2/_3$ yd. white fabric (Blocks)

$1^1/_4$ yds. dark pink fabric (Blocks and Binding)

1 yd. pink print fabric (Outer Border)

BATTING AND BACKING YARDAGE

Twin size batting

Backing (choose one):

42" wide fabric: $3^3/_8$ yds.
90" wide fabric: $1^3/_4$ yds.
108" wide fabric: $1^3/_4$ yds.

CUTTING INSTRUCTIONS

For Fat Quarter Quilt Only

Using the Fat Quarter Cutting Diagram as a guide, cut from each fat quarter:

(4) $2^1/_2$" jelly roll strips.

(1) $4^1/_2$" charm square strip; subcut into $4^1/_2$" squares.

Follow the instructions below for subcutting pre-cuts and cutting additional yardage.

For Pre-Cuts and Fat Quarter Quilts

Trim each charm square to $4^1/_2$" square.

Cut 12 jelly roll strips each into 4 equal segments (approximately $10^1/_2$"–11" long).

From the white fabric, cut (14) $1^1/_2$" strips for the Four Patches.

From the dark pink fabric, cut:

(14) $1^1/_2$" strips for the Four Patches.

$2^1/_2$" strips for binding.

From the pink print fabric, cut (7) $4^1/_2$" strips for the Outer Border.

Fat Quarter Cutting Diagram

SEWING INSTRUCTIONS

Follow the block instructions for MIXED FRUIT SORBET (pages 60–61) to make and assemble forty-eight blocks, but use the same fabric in the jelly roll pieces of the Ten-Patch units as the charm squares.

ASSEMBLING THE QUILT TOP

1. Lay out the blocks according to the Quilt Layout (page 64), six blocks across by eight rows down.

2. Sew each row of blocks together. Press seams on even rows one way and odd rows the other way.

3. Sew the rows together to complete the inner quilt top. Press.

ADDING THE BORDER

1. Measure the quilt from top to bottom in several places and average the results. Piece together and cut border strips to that length. Sew one strip to each side of the quilt. Press the seams toward this border.

2. Measure the quilt from side to side in several places and average the results. Piece together and cut border strips to that length. Sew these strips to the top and bottom of the quilt. Press the seams toward this border.

Layer and quilt, bind and enjoy!

Layer Cake Charm

If you want to whip up a decent-sized quilt in a jiffy or if you're a beginner, this is the quilt for you. You'll have a lot of fun arranging the blocks and playing with the wash of colors. This is one poppin', rockin' girlie quilt!

Quilt Size: 79" × 79" (Double/Full)

Block Size: 9" × 9"

Pieced by Amy Greenway, quilted by Bobbi Lang.

Choosing Fabrics

I used the Moda *Happy* pre-cut line for this quilt. If it's not available, choose pre-cuts that feature children's or novelty prints. Focus on yellow, pink and green, with black accents. Or use any line that has a spectrum of contrasting colors. Purchase additional yardage as specified in colors that coordinate with your particular pre-cut line.

This Quilt's Pre-Cuts...

layer cake • charm squares

MATERIALS

FOR PRE-CUTS QUILT

1 layer cake (Blocks)

(56) 5" charm squares (Border 2)

Additional yardage

FOR FAT QUARTER QUILT

1 fat quarter bundle or at least 18 coordinating fat quarters (Blocks and Border 2)

Additional yardage

ADDITIONAL YARDAGE

¾ yd. coordinating fabric 1 (Border 1)

1⅛ yds. coordinating fabric 2 (Border 3 and Binding)

1¼ yds. coordinating fabric 3 (Border 4)

BATTING AND BACKING YARDAGE

Queen size batting

Backing (choose one):

42" wide fabric: 4⅔ yds.
90" wide fabric: 2⅜ yds.
108" wide fabric: 2⅜ yds.

CUTTING INSTRUCTIONS

For Fat Quarter Quilt Only

Using the Fat Quarter Cutting Diagram as a guide, cut from each fat quarter:

(1) 10" wide layer cake strip; subcut into (2) 10" squares.

(1) 5" wide charm square strip; subcut into 5" squares.

Follow the instructions below for subcutting pre-cuts and cutting additional yardage.

For Pre-Cuts and Fat Quarter Quilts

Trim 36 of the layer cake squares to 9½" square.

From the Border 1 fabric, cut (6) 3½" wide strips; subcut 2 of the strips in half to equal about 21" long.

From the Border 3 fabric, cut (8) 1½" wide strips; subcut the rest of the fabric into 2½" wide bias strips for binding.

From the Border 4 fabric, cut (8) 5" wide strips.

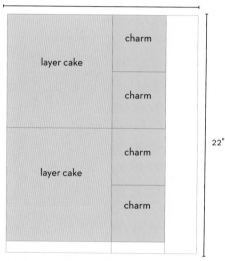

Fat Quarter Cutting Diagram

SEWING INSTRUCTIONS

1. Arrange the layer cake squares into six rows of six blocks each, creating balance throughout the top by distributing the colors and patterns randomly. Adjust them until you are pleased with the balance.

2. Sew the blocks into rows. Press odd-row seam allowances to the left and even-row seam allowances to the right. (Figure 1)

3. Sew the rows together, pressing the rows in one direction. (Figure 2)

ADDING THE BORDERS

Border 1

1. Sew each long strip of 3½" fabric end-to-end with a short strip of fabric. Press.

2. Measure the quilt from top to bottom in several places. Average the lengths and cut two of the pieced strips to that length.

3. Sew one strip to each side of the top. Press toward this border.

4. Measure the top from side to side in several places. Average that length and cut the two remaining pieced strips to that length.

5. Sew one strip to the top and the other to the bottom of the quilt. Press toward this border. (Figure 3)

6. Square up the quilt to exactly 59" square so the charm square border in the next steps will fit correctly.

Sew You Know . . .

Try "checker-boarding" warm (red, orange, yellow) and cool (green, blue, purple) colors. Avoid putting like colors and prints next to each other.

Figure 1

Figure 2

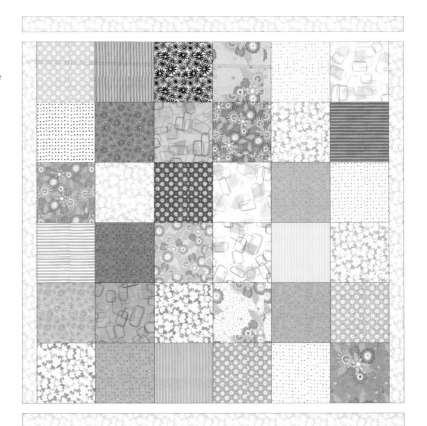

Figure 3

Border 2

1. Arrange the charm squares around the outside of the quilt top in a manner that is pleasing to you.

2. Sew thirteen blocks together to form the left side border. Press in one direction. Repeat to form the right side border.

3. Sew each side border to the quilt top. Press toward Border 1. (Figure 4)

4. Sew fifteen blocks together to form the top border. Press in one direction. Repeat to form the bottom border.

5. Sew the border strips to the top and bottom of the quilt. Press toward Border 1. (Figure 4)

Border 3

1. Sew four of the long strips of 1½" fabric end-to-end with the other four strips. Press.

2. Continue as for Border 1, steps 2–5.

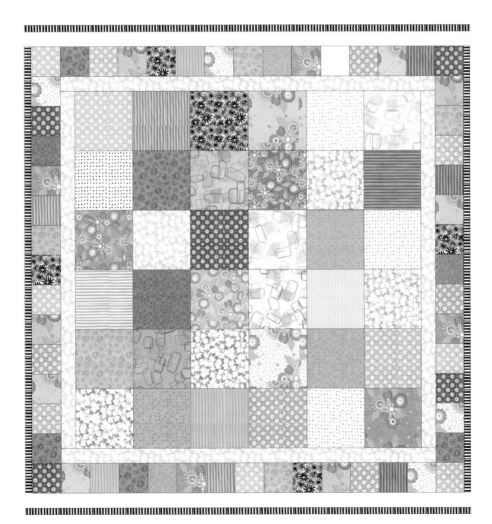

Figure 4

Border 4

1. Sew four of the long strips of 5" fabric end-to-end with the other four strips. Press.

2. For each side border, measure the quilt from top to bottom in several places. Average the results and cut two of the 5" pieced border strips that length.

3. Sew one of the side strips to each side of the quilt. Press the seams toward Border 3.

4. For the top and bottom borders, measure the quilt from side to side in several places. Average the results and subtract 9" (to accommodate the charm square corners). Cut the other two 5" border strips that length.

5. Sew a charm square to each end of these two border strips. Press toward the border strips. Sew these borders to the top and bottom of the quilt. Press the seams toward Border 3.

Layer and quilt, bind and enjoy!

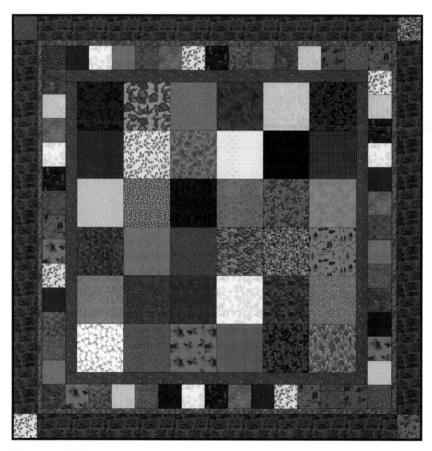

Alternate Colorway

Quilt Layout

Log Cabin Schoolhouse

Prairie points are a natural for charm squares—they're so easy, and they really complement the Log Cabin setting triangles. The seven pieced blocks are also a great setting for other types of blocks, like days-of-the-week embroidery or sampler-style blocks.

Quilt Size: 42" × 54¾" with prairie points (Crib/Throw)

Block Size: 8" × 8"

Pieced and quilted by the author.

Choosing Fabrics

I used the *Punctuation* pre-cut line by Moda for this quilt. If it's not available, choose pre-cuts that feature primary colors, especially blue and yellow with black and white. Or use any line that has bright, small prints. Purchase additional yardage as specified in colors that coordinate with your particular pre-cut line.

- -

This Quilt's Pre-Cuts...

honey bun • charm squares

MATERIALS

FOR PRE-CUTS QUILT

1 honey bun (Blocks, Sashing and Borders)

(42) 5" charm squares (Prairie Points)

Additional yardage

FOR FAT QUARTER QUILT

1 fat quarter bundle or at least 14 coordinating fat quarters (Blocks, Borders and Prairie Points)

Additional yardage

ADDITIONAL YARDAGE

³⁄₈ yd. white fabric (Block Background)

¹⁄₂ yd. orange print fabric (Logs, Border 3 and Prairie Points)

⁵⁄₈ yd. yellow print fabric (Setting Triangles, Logs, Sashing, Border 1 and Prairie Points)

¹⁄₂ yd. dark blue print fabric (Border 4 and Prairie Points)

¹⁄₂ yd. red print fabric (Border 2 and Prairie Points)

BATTING AND BACKING YARDAGE

Crib/throw size batting

Backing (choose one):

42" wide fabric: 1⁵⁄₈ yds.

90" wide fabric: 1¹⁄₄ yds.

108" wide fabric: 1¹⁄₄ yds.

CUTTING INSTRUCTIONS

For Fat Quarter Quilt Only

Using the Fat Quarter Cutting Diagram as a guide, cut from each fat quarter:

(6) 1¹⁄₂" wide honey bun strips.

(1) 5" wide charm square strip; subcut into 5" squares.

Follow the instructions below for subcutting pre-cuts and cutting additional yardage.

For Pre-Cuts and Fat Quarter Quilts

From dark blue honey bun strips, cut (28) 1¹⁄₂" × 2¹⁄₂" rectangles in groups of 4 from each print for the Center blocks.

From black honey bun strips, cut (28) 1¹⁄₂" squares in groups of 4 from each print for the Center blocks.

From the orange honey bun strips, cut (18) 1¹⁄₂" corner squares for sashing.

From the white fabric, cut (4) 2¹⁄₂" strips for the Center blocks; subcut into (28) 2¹⁄₂" × 4¹⁄₂" rectangles.

From the orange print fabric, cut:

(1) 3¹⁄₄" wide strip; subcut into (3) 3¹⁄₄" squares for the setting triangles.

(3) 1¹⁄₂" wide strips; subcut 1 strip in half to approximately 21" long for Border 3.

From the yellow print fabric, cut:

(1) 3¹⁄₄" wide strip; subcut into (3) 3¹⁄₄" squares for the setting triangles.

(6) 1¹⁄₂" strips; subcut into (24) 1¹⁄₂" × 8¹⁄₂" rectangles for sashing.

(4) 1¹⁄₂" wide strips; subcut (2) 38¹⁄₂" long strips and (2) 28¹⁄₂" long strips for Border 1.

From the dark blue print fabric, cut (5) 2¹⁄₂" wide strips for Border 4.

From the red print fabric, cut:

(1) 2¹⁄₂" strip; subcut into (7) 2¹⁄₂" squares for the Center blocks.

(2) 2¹⁄₂" wide strips; subcut (2) 30¹⁄₂" long strips for Border 2.

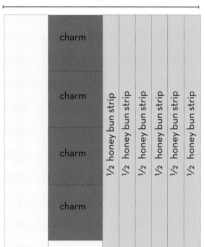

Fat Quarter Cutting Diagram

SEWING INSTRUCTIONS

Corner Four Patches (Make 28)

1. From the honey bun strips, choose seven warm-colored (e.g., orange) strips and seven cool-colored (e.g., green) strips. Cut about 12" off each strip and return the rest to the honey bun stack.

2. Sew an orange 12" strip to each green 12" strip along one long edge. Press toward the green strip. (Figure 1)

3. Crosscut eight 1½" units from each strip set. You will need seven matching sets of eight units each. (Figure 2)

4. From each group of eight crosscut units, turn four upside down. Sew each upside-down unit to a right-side-up unit to make a Four Patch square. Press to the side. (Figure 3)

5. For each of the seven center blocks, gather together four matching Four Patches, four matching white rectangles, four matching black squares, four matching dark blue rectangles and a red print square.

Center Nine Patches (Make 7)

1. Sew a blue rectangle to each side of the seven red squares. Press toward the blue. (Figure 4)

2. Sew a black square to both short ends of each remaining blue rectangle. Press toward the blue. (Figure 5)

3. Sew a blue-black unit to both long edges of a red-blue unit to make a Nine Patch. Press toward the blue. (Figure 6)

4. Sew a white rectangle to two opposite sides of each Nine Patch. Press toward the blue. (Figure 7)

Figure 1

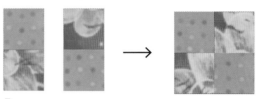

Figure 2

Figure 3

Figure 4

Figure 5

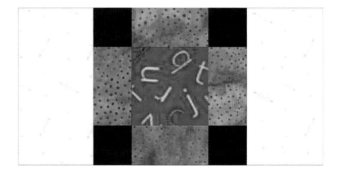

Figure 6

Figure 7

5. Sew a Four Patch to both short ends of each remaining white rectangle, using Figure 8 as a guide for the Four Patch color orientation. Press toward the Four Patch.

6. Sew one of the units from step 5 to the top and bottom of each unit from step 4. Use Figure 9 as a guide for the Four Patch color orientation. Press toward the center.

MAKING THE SETTING TRIANGLES

Center Triangle

1. Draw a diagonal line from corner to corner on the back of each of the three 3¼" yellow print squares. (Figure 10)

2. Place each yellow square right sides together with an orange square. (Figure 11)

3. Sew ¼" on either side of the drawn line. (Figure 12)

4. Cut along the drawn line. Press. (Figure 13)

5. Open up each triangle and press the seam allowances toward the orange side. Now you have six triangle squares. (Figure 14)

6. Cut these squares in half diagonally the opposite way. (Figure 15) The sides should measure 2" long.

7. You have twelve triangles, but you will only need ten. Choose five of each configuration.

Figure 8

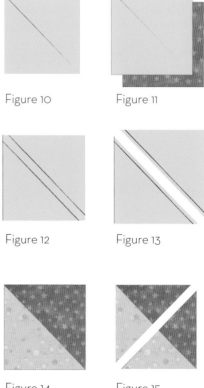

Figure 9

Figure 10   Figure 11

Figure 12   Figure 13

Figure 14   Figure 15

Log Strips (Make 10)

1. Place a setting triangle right-side-up with the right angle in the upper right corner. (Figure 16)

2. Place a black honey bun strip right-side-down, lining it up with the corner and the right edge of the triangle. Sew along this side.

3. Trim the honey bun strip about 2" past the bottom of the triangle edge. Press. Open up the piece and press toward the strip. Make ten. (Figure 17)

4. Place the second black honey bun strip right sides together with the other short edge of the triangle, the end of the new strip even with the edge of the first strip. Sew along the edge of the new strip.

5. Trim the strip about 2" past the bottom of the triangle edge. Press. Open up the piece and press toward the strip. (Figure 18)

6. Continue adding strips in the same manner for two more rounds, leaving about 2" more fabric than on each previous round. First use the red strips, then the blue and green strips in the final round. Use the illustration as a placement guide. (Figure 19)

Figure 16   Figure 17   Figure 18

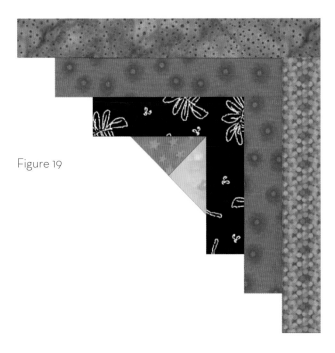

Figure 19

ADDING THE SASHING

1. Lay out the quilt top as desired, using the Quilt Layout (page 81) as a reference.

2. Place sashing strips between each block and between the blocks and setting triangles. (Figure 20)

3. Place a corner square at the intersection of each sashing strip and around the edges where the sashing strips end. (Figure 20)

4. Starting in the upper left corner, stitch a corner block to the sashing strip. Then stitch a setting triangle to each side of the sashing strip, lining up the blue or green edges with the end of the sashing strip. Press the seams toward the sashing strip.

5. Next, sew the first diagonal sashing row. Press the seams toward the sashing strips. (Figure 21)

6. Sew the sashing strip to the corner unit, right sides together, matching the center corner square of the sashing to the center sashing strip of the corner unit. Press toward the sashing. (Figure 22)

7. Continue on in this manner, stitching the blocks for each diagonal row together. Sew the rows together to form the quilt top.

8. Finally, lay the quilt top out on a cutting mat and trim off all the edges to square up the top. Be sure to leave a $\frac{1}{4}$" seam allowance on all four sides. The quilt top should measure $26\frac{1}{2}$" × $38\frac{1}{2}$".

Figure 20

Figure 21

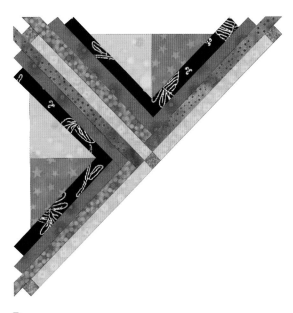

Figure 22

77

ADDING THE BORDERS

Border 1 (Yellow Print)

1. Sew the two $38\frac{1}{2}"$ strips to each side of the quilt top. Press the seams toward the borders.

2. Sew the two $28\frac{1}{2}"$ strips to the top and bottom of the quilt top. Press the seams toward the borders. Be sure the quilt top now measures $40\frac{1}{2}" \times 28\frac{1}{2}"$. (Figure 23)

Border 2 (Red Print and Checkerboard)

1. Using the honey bun strips, pair up each dark strip with a light strip. If you do not have an even number of each, that is okay; just do not pair up two similar fabrics.

2. With right sides together, sew the pairs together along one long side. Press the seams toward the darker color. (Figure 24)

3. Crosscut the strips into $1\frac{1}{2}"$ units. (Figure 25)

4. Mixing up all the units, join enough of them side to side into strips to make two borders, one forty squares long and the other forty-four squares long. (Figure 26)

5. Set the remaining crosscut units aside for Border 3.

6. Sew the shorter checkerboard border to the left side of the quilt. Press the seam toward Border 1.

7. Sew the $30\frac{1}{2}"$ red print strips to the top and bottom of the quilt. Press the seams toward Border 1.

8. Sew the longer checkerboard border to the right side of the quilt. Press the seam toward Border 1. Be sure the quilt top now measures $32\frac{1}{2}" \times 44\frac{1}{2}"$.

Figure 23

Figure 24

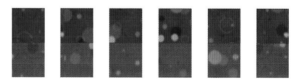

Figure 25

Figure 26

Sew You Know . . .

It is really easy to sew the borders to the bias edges of the quilt top if you sew with the borders on top. Pin the borders onto the top every few inches, and the feed dogs of the machine will ease those edges right into place!

Border 3 (Orange Print and Checkerboard)

1. Sew one short orange print strip to the end of each of two long strips. Trim one strip to 44½" long and the other strip to 46½" long.

2. Sew the shorter orange print strip to the left side of the quilt top. Press the seams toward this border.

3. Retrieve the remaining crosscut honey bun units and sew them together end-to-end to create two borders one unit wide. Both strips should be thirty-three units long.

4. Sew the checkerboard borders to the top and bottom of the quilt. Press the seams toward Border 2.

5. Sew the longer orange print strip to the right side of the quilt top. Press the seam toward this border.

Border 4 (Dark Blue Print)

1. Cut one of the dark blue 2½" border strips in half to equal about 21" long.

2. Sew one of the dark blue 2½" × 21" border strips to one end of each of two long blue strips.

3. For each side border, measure the quilt from top to bottom in several places. Average the results and cut the two long border strips that length. Sew one strip to each side of the quilt. Press the seams toward this border.

4. For the top and bottom borders, measure the quilt from side to side in several places. Average the results and cut the two short blue border strips that length. Sew these strips to the top and bottom of the quilt. Press the seams toward this border. (Figure 27)

Figure 27

CHARM SQUARE PRAIRIE POINTS

1. From leftover yardage, cut enough 5" squares so that, with the charm pack, you have forty-eight 5" squares.

2. With right sides out, fold the squares in half diagonally. Fold them in half again diagonally and press. (Figure 28)

3. With the quilt top laid flat, arrange the prairie points along the edges. You should have fourteen on each side and ten across the top and bottom. Tuck all the overlapping edges inside the next point, keeping the folded edges in the same position as you turn corners.

4. Pin the prairie points in place on the quilt top, raw edges together and with the points toward the middle. Sew in place ¼" from the edge. (Figure 29)

5. Quilt the top, lifting the prairie points out of the way as needed. Do not quilt out farther than ½" from the edge.

6. Once the top is quilted, trim the backing of the quilt even with the raw edge of the top. Carefully lift the top and trim the batting back ¼". Point the prairie points outward, turning the raw edge inside. Press.

7. Turn under the raw edge of the backing ¼" and stitch it down by hand.

8. Topstitch through all the layers close to the edge of the quilt. Enjoy!

Figure 28

Figure 29

Alternate Colorway

Quilt Layout

Kansas Harvest Fields

This quilt reminds me of the way country fields jump to life when the sun breaks through dark clouds after a rain. The colors are rich and dark, but the careful placement of the lights really brings out the deep hues.

Quilt Size: 64" × 84" (Twin)

Block Size: 6" × 6"

Pieced by the author, quilted by Bobbi Lang.

Choosing Fabrics

I used the *Kansas Troubles Butterfly Garden* Moda pre-cut line for this quilt. You will find that you may substitute just about any current line of *Kansas Troubles* pre-cuts. Or use any line that has a spectrum of darkly muted, primitive country colors. Purchase additional yardage as specified in colors that coordinate with your particular pre-cut line.

- -

This Quilt's Pre-Cuts...

jelly roll • honey bun

MATERIALS

FOR PRE-CUTS QUILT

1 jelly roll (Blocks)

1 honey bun (Sashing)

Additional yardage

FOR FAT QUARTER QUILT

1 fat quarter bundle or at least 10 coordinating fat quarters (Blocks and Sashing)

Additional yardage

ADDITIONAL YARDAGE

$\frac{5}{8}$ yd. burgundy fabric (Pieced Border)

1 yd. dark green fabric (Narrow Border and Binding)

$2\frac{1}{2}$ yds. copper floral fabric (Plain Blocks, Setting Triangles and Outer Border)

BATTING AND BACKING YARDAGE

Double/full size batting

Backing (choose one):

42" wide fabric: 5 yds.
90" wide fabric: 2 yds.
108" wide fabric: 2 yds.

CUTTING INSTRUCTIONS

For Fat Quarter Quilt Only

Using the Fat Quarter Cutting Diagram as a guide, cut from each fat quarter:

(4) $1\frac{1}{2}$" wide honey bun strips.

(4) $2\frac{1}{2}$" wide jelly roll strips.

Follow the instructions below for cutting additional yardage.

For Pre-Cuts and Fat Quarter Quilts

Cut each jelly roll strip in half to equal about 21" long.

To make the Plain blocks, cut (3) $6\frac{1}{2}$" strips from the copper floral fabric. Subcut into (12) $6\frac{1}{2}$" squares. Set aside the rest of the strips for the corner setting triangles.

To make the side setting triangles, cut (2) $9\frac{3}{4}$" strips from the copper floral fabric. Subcut these into (5) $9\frac{3}{4}$" squares. Cut each square in half diagonally from corner to corner twice.

To make the corner setting triangles, cut (2) $5\frac{1}{8}$" squares from the remainder of the copper floral fabric strips you cut earlier. Cut each square in half diagonally from corner to corner once.

From the dark green yardage, cut:

(7) $1\frac{1}{2}$" strips for the Narrow Border.

$2\frac{1}{2}$" strips for binding.

From the copper floral yardage, cut (13) $2\frac{1}{2}$" strips for the Outer Border.

From the burgundy yardage, cut (7) $2\frac{1}{2}$" strips for the Outer Border.

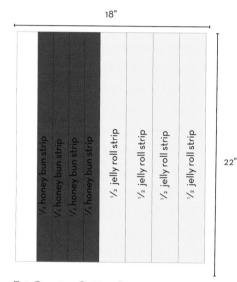

Fat Quarter Cutting Diagram

SEWING INSTRUCTIONS

For each color grouping of Nine Patch blocks, follow these instructions:

1. To make one set of three Nine Patch blocks, match up two Color A and two coordinating Color B 21" jelly roll strips.

2. Trim two A strips and one B strip to about 16" long. Set the cutoff pieces aside.

3. Sew the three 16" strips together with the B strip in the middle, making an ABA unit. Press toward the darker strip. (Figure 1)

4. Crosscut the strip into six 2½" ABA units. (Figure 2)

5. Cut the remaining 21" B strip in thirds, each piece about 7" long.

6. Match two of these short B strips with both leftover short A strips.

7. Sew these units together with the A strip in the middle to make two short BAB strip sets. Press toward the darker strip. (Figure 3)

8. Crosscut the units into three 2½" BAB units. You will need only three. (Figure 4)

9. To make three Nine Patch blocks, stitch an ABA unit to each side of the BAB units. Press. (Figure 5)

Follow the above instructions to make Nine Patches in the following color combinations:

Red and Blue Nine Patches (Make 19)

You will need fourteen red (A) strips and fourteen blue (B) strips.

Green and Plum Nine Patches (Make 16)

You will need twelve green (A) strips and fourteen plum (B) strips.

Beige and Gold Nine Patches (Make 16)

1. You will need twelve beige (A) strips and twelve gold (B) strips.

2. Set aside four of the blocks for the Outer Border.

Figure 1

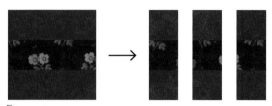

Figure 2

Figure 3

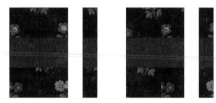

Figure 4

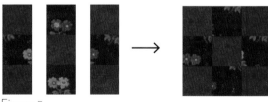

Figure 5

ADDING THE SASHING

1. Lay out the Nine Patches, setting triangles and Plain blocks as desired, leaving about 1" between blocks. Use the Quilt Layout (page 87) as a reference for placement.

2. Place honey bun strips in the rows between the blocks and setting triangles until you find an arrangement you like.

3. From the honey bun strips, cut 6½" pieces. (Each honey bun strip can yield six pieces.) Place the pieces back in their location immediately after cutting each strip.

4. In the same manner, choose which fabrics you wish to use for sashing corner squares. Remember you will also need sashing squares where the strips end at the edges of the quilt.

5. From the leftover honey bun strips, cut 1½" corner squares and place them where they belong on the quilt top. Each honey bun strip can yield twenty-eight squares.

6. Starting in the upper left corner of the quilt, sew sashing corner blocks to both ends of the first sashing strip. Sew the sashing strip to the setting triangle. (Figure 6)

7. Sew the upper left side setting triangle to a sashing strip. Then stitch that unit to the Nine Patch block. Sew that unit to the next sashing strip, and finally to the top-side setting triangle. (Figure 7)

8. Sew diagonal rows together, placing sashing strips and cornerstones where necessary.

9. Lay the quilt top on a cutting mat and trim off all the sashing square edges to square up the top. Be sure to leave a ¼" seam allowance.

Figure 6

Figure 7

Sew You Know . . .

• After you lay out the quilt top, take a picture with a digital camera to help you remember the block and sashing placement.

• Always press toward the sashing strip and away from the blocks and corner squares for less bulk.

ADDING THE BORDERS

Narrow Border (Green)

1. Measure the quilt from top to bottom in several places and average the results. Piece and cut two green border strips to that length.

2. Sew the two pieced strips to the sides of the quilt top. Press toward the border.

3. Measure the quilt from side to side in several places and average the results. Piece and cut two green border strips to that length.

4. Sew the two pieced strips to the top and bottom of the quilt top. Press toward the border.

Outer Border

1. Sew the 2½" copper floral strips end-to-end. Do the same with the burgundy strips.

2. Cut the long copper floral strip in half, creating two pieces, each approximately 273" long. Sew a copper floral strip to each side of the burgundy strip. Press.

3. Measure the quilt again from top to bottom in several places and average the results.

4. Measure the quilt from side to side in several places and average the results.

5. Cut two copper-burgundy-copper units the length you calculated in step 3. Sew one unit to each side of the quilt.

6. Cut two more copper-burgundy-copper units the length you calculated in step 4. Sew a beige and gold Nine Patch block to each end of these units. Sew them to the top and bottom of the quilt. Press.

Layer and quilt, bind and enjoy!

Alternate Colorway

Quilt Layout

Not the Old-School Way

Wonder what would happen if...? Try something new! I took a perfectly good cross-shaped block and whacked off all four corners, leaving me with a nifty diagonal cross and triangular corners with little tips that were too cool to ignore! Not exactly the old-school way of coming up with an old-school look!

Quilt Size: 81" × 104" (Full/Queen with Pillow Tuck)

Block Size: 11½" × 11½"

Pieced by Diana Snyder and the author, quilted by Bobbi Lang.

Choosing Fabrics

I used Moda's *Le Petite Ecole* and *Antique Fair* pre-cut lines for this quilt. Pre-cuts that feature grayed colors, such as Williamsburg blue and Turkey red, or a line of Civil War reproduction fabrics would also work very well. Purchase additional yardage as specified in colors that coordinate with your particular pre-cut line. Frequently one manufacturer will share the same colorways from line to line, sometimes even designer to designer, as in this case. This is one of the beauties of pre-cuts—easy combining opportunities! Makes it handy for us, doesn't it?

- -

This Quilt's Pre-Cuts...

jelly roll • charm squares • layer cake

MATERIALS

FOR PRE-CUTS QUILT

1 jelly roll (Blocks and Scrappy Binding)

42 pairs of identical 5" charm squares, for a total of 84 squares (Blocks)

1 layer cake (Plain Blocks)

Additional yardage

FOR FAT QUARTER QUILT

1 fat quarter bundle or at least 40 coordinating fat quarters (Blocks, Pieced Border)

Additional yardage

ADDITIONAL YARDAGE

1⅛ yds. red fabric (Borders 1 and 3)

2 yds. beige print fabric (Borders 2 and 4)

¾ yd. red and brown stripe fabric (Binding)

BATTING AND BACKING YARDAGE

King size batting

Backing (choose one):

42" wide fabric: 7⅛ yds.
90" wide fabric: 3 yds.
108" wide fabric: 3 yds.

CUTTING INSTRUCTIONS

For Fat Quarter Quilt Only

Using the Fat Quarter Cutting Diagram as a guide, cut from each fat quarter:

(1) 10" strip; subcut into 1 pile of 10" layer cake squares and 2 piles of 5" charm squares. From the remaining fabric in the 10" strip, cut 8" × 2½" strips for block frames.

(3) 2½" jelly roll strips; subcut 20 strips into 2½" squares for blocks; subcut 18 strips into 5" strips for blocks; subcut 30 strips into 8" strips for block frames.

Follow the instructions below for cutting additional yardage.

For Pre-Cuts Quilt Only

From the layer cake, cut (17) 8" squares for alternating blocks, starting with the largest prints. Subcut the remaining 23 blocks into 8" × 2½" strips for block frames.

From 21 jelly roll strips, cut (2) 2½" squares, (4) 5" lengths and (2) 8" lengths. From each of the 21 remaining strips, subcut (4) 8" lengths and (3) 2½" squares for the Cross blocks and block frames.

From 12 charm squares, cut (4) 2½" squares for blocks and block frames.

For Pre-Cuts and Fat Quarter Quilts

From the red fabric, cut (7) 1½" strips for Border 1 and (9) 2½" strips for Border 3.

From the beige print fabric, cut (5) 5⅜" strips for Border 2 and (9) 4" strips for Border 4.

From the brown and red stripe fabric, cut 2½" bias strips for binding.

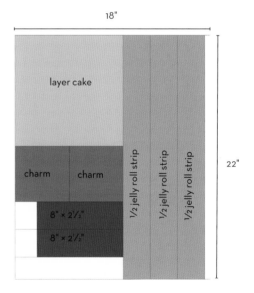

Fat Quarter Cutting Diagram

Note: The following instructions use 42" long jelly roll strips. If you use fat quarters, double the number of strips in the instructions. For example, ten jelly roll strips equal twenty fat quarter strips.

SEWING INSTRUCTIONS

Cross Blocks (Make 18)

1. For each of the eighteen Cross blocks, gather two pairs of two coordinating charm squares, one $2\frac{1}{2}$" square, and four identical $2\frac{1}{2}$" × 5" rectangles. (Figure 1)

2. Lay out the pieces as shown in Figure 2 and assemble them row by row. Press. The block should measure $11\frac{1}{2}$" square.

3. Measure and mark the center point of each edge of the block.

4. Cut off the corners of each block by cutting from the center of each edge to the center of the adjacent edge. (Figure 3)

5. Set the triangles aside for the border. Trim the resulting blocks to 8" square.

Figure 1

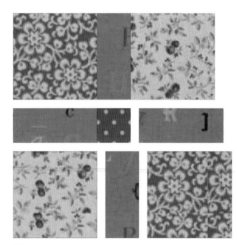

Figure 2

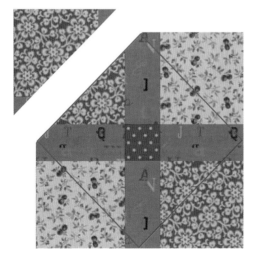

Figure 3

FRAMING THE BLOCKS

1. For each of the eighteen Cross blocks and seventeen Plain blocks, gather four coordinating 8" strips and four coordinating 2½" squares. (Figure 4)

2. Lay out the pieces and assemble them row by row. Press. (Figure 5)

3. Trim the blocks to 12" square.

ASSEMBLING THE QUILT TOP

1. Lay out the blocks according to the Quilt Layout (page 93), five blocks across by seven rows down. Start with a Cross block in the upper left corner and alternate across and down with Plain blocks.

2. Sew each row of blocks together. Press seams on the even rows one way and the odd rows the other way.

3. Sew the rows together to complete the inner quilt top. Press. The quilt top should measure 58" × 81".

MAKING THE BORDERS

Border 1 (Red)

1. Cut and piece two 1½" red strips, both 81" long. Sew one to each side of the quilt. Press toward the border.

2. Cut and piece two 1½" red strips, both 60" long and sew them to the top and bottom of the quilt. Press toward the border.

Border 2 (Pieced)

1. To create the triangle blocks in the border, assemble twenty-eight half-triangle squares from fifty-six of the cut-off Cross block corners. With right sides together, sew long edge to long edge. Press. Trim each to 5⅜" square. (Figure 6)

2. Lay out the border squares using the Quilt Layout as a reference.

3. Sew the blocks together, for one edge of the quilt at a time. For instance, stitch the two in the upper left corner together. Then stitch the five in the upper right corner together, followed by the four in the upper right side border, and so on. You will be stitching the corner blocks to the top and bottom red borders. Press.

Figure 4

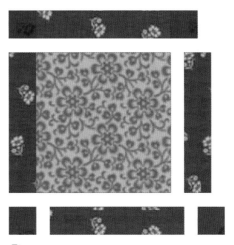

Figure 5

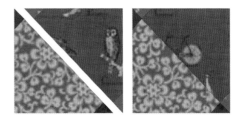

Figure 6

4. To assemble the left side border, stitch two of the 5⅜" beige border strips together and cut it to 53¾" long. Sew the one half-square triangle block to the top of the strip and the five half-square triangle blocks to the bottom. Watch the block orientation carefully. Press. (Figure 7)

5. For the right side border, stitch a beige border strip to the rest of the border strip you cut off in step 4. Cut it to 48⅞" long. Sew the four half-square triangle blocks to the top of the strip and the three half-square triangle blocks to the bottom. Press. (Figure 8)

6. For the top border, cut a beige border strip to 35¾" long. Sew the two half-square triangle blocks to the left side and the five half-square triangle blocks to the right side. Press. (Figure 9)

7. For the bottom border, cut the remaining beige border strip to 30¾" long. Sew the five half-square triangle blocks to the left side and the three half-square triangle blocks to the right side. Press. (Figure 10)

8. Sew the side borders to the sides of the quilt top. Press toward Border 1. Sew the top and bottom borders to the quilt top. Press toward Border 1.

Border 3 (Red)

1. Measure the quilt from top to bottom in several places and average the results. Piece and cut two 2½" red border strips to that length. Sew these strips to the sides of the quilt. Press toward this border.

2. Measure the quilt again from side to side in several places and average the results. Piece and cut two more 2½" strips to that length. Sew these strips to the top and bottom of the quilt. Press toward this border.

Border 4 (Beige)

In the same way as for Border 3, measure and sew on 4" beige borders to complete the quilt top.

Layer and quilt, bind and enjoy!

Figure 9

Figure 10

Figure 7   Figure 8

Alternate Colorway

Quilt Layout

Pre-Cuts Potpourri

This simple pieced quilt can have a plethora of personalities depending on the fabrics you choose. Mix up all your pre-cuts into a delightful potpourri of colorful blocks. It goes so fast and is so much fun!

Quilt Size: 80" × 91"
(Double/Full)

Block Size: 9" × 9"

Pieced and quilted by the author.

Choosing Fabrics

I used the *Rural Jardin* Moda pre-cut line for this quilt. Moda's French General designers frequently introduce similar colorways you may use. Or use any line that has an assortment of somewhat grayed colors. Purchase additional yardage as specified in colors that coordinate with your particular pre-cut line.

This Quilt's Pre-Cuts...

layer cake • charm squares • jelly roll

MATERIALS

FOR PRE-CUTS QUILT

1 layer cake (Blocks)

14 pairs of identical 5" charm squares, for a total of 28 squares (Blocks)

1 jelly roll (Blocks)

Additional yardage

FOR FAT QUARTER QUILT

1 fat quarter bundle or at least 35 coordinating fat quarters (Blocks)

Additional yardage

ADDITIONAL YARDAGE

2½ yds. coordinating fabric (Outer Border)

¾ yds. coordinating fabric (Binding)

BATTING AND BACKING YARDAGE

Queen size batting

Backing (choose one):

42" wide fabric: 7 yds.
90" wide fabric: 2¾ yds.
108" wide fabric: 2⅓ yds.

CUTTING INSTRUCTIONS

For Fat Quarter Quilt Only

Using the Fat Quarter Cutting Diagram as a guide, cut from each fat quarter:

(3) 2½" wide jelly roll strips.

(1) 10" wide layer cake strip; subcut into 10" squares.

Cut the remainder of the fat quarter into (4) 5" charm squares.

Follow the instructions below for subcutting pre-cuts and cutting additional yardage.

For Pre-Cuts and Fat Quarter Quilts

From the layer cake, separate out 19 of the largest prints, tone-on-tones and solids. Trim these 19 to exactly 9½" square for whole blocks.

From the remaining 21 layer cake squares (mostly small prints), cut:

(2) 3½" strips; subcut into (81) 3½" squares for Nine Patch blocks.

(1) 2¾" strip. Subcut 20 strips to 9½" long for Rail Fence blocks. Subcut the remaining strip into (32) 2¾" squares for Sixteen Patch blocks.

From the jelly roll, separate out 4 of the solid and tone-on-tone fabrics. From these 4 strips, subcut (56) 2½" squares for sashing corner squares.

From the remaining jelly roll strips, cut out at least (97) 2½" × 9½" strips for sashing.

From the coordinating fabric Outer Border yardage, cut (4) 6½" wide strips by the length of the fabric.

Cut 2½" strips from the binding fabric.

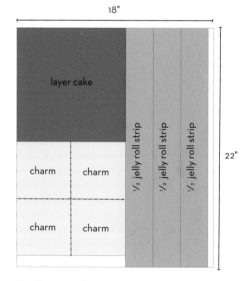

Fat Quarter Cutting Diagram

SEWING INSTRUCTIONS

Four Patch Blocks (Make 7)

1. Pair up each charm square with its matching charm square from the other pack.

2. From the paired charm squares, pair up sets of four charm squares.

3. Stitch each pair of squares to its coordinate and press the seams toward the darker fabric. (Figure 1)

4. Turn one pair upside down and join it to its partner to make the Four Patch block. Press. (Figure 2)

5. Trim the Four Patch blocks to measure exactly $9\frac{1}{2}$" square.

Rail Fence Block (Make 5)

1. Divide your twenty $2\frac{3}{4}$" × $9\frac{1}{2}$" strips into five piles of four strips each.

2. Stitch each pile of four strips together to make each block. Press. (Figure 3)

3. Trim the Rail Fence blocks to measure exactly $9\frac{1}{2}$" square.

Nine Patch Blocks (Make 9)

1. From your (81) $3\frac{1}{2}$" squares, arrange nine Nine Patch blocks. According to your particular mix of fabrics, you may be able to match up four darks, four lights and one accent for a center block, or arrange any other combination you like.

2. Arrange the squares into the configuration you want. Stitch the squares into three rows of three blocks each. Press the two like rows in one direction and the row with the center block in the other direction. (Figure 4)

3. Stitch the rows together to complete the Nine Patch. Press. (Figure 5)

4. Trim the Nine Patch blocks to measure exactly $9\frac{1}{2}$" square.

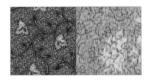

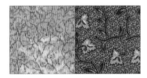

Figure 1

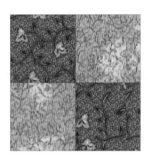

Figure 2

Figure 3

Figure 4

Figure 5

Sixteen Patch Blocks (Make 2)

1. Gather up all of the 2¾" squares. Randomly choosing your patches, chainstitch them together in groups of two. Press. (Figure 6)

2. Randomly choosing your groups, chainstitch them together end-to-end to make eight rows of four patches each. Press the seams in the same direction. (Figure 7)

3. Place two rows right sides together with seam allowances facing in opposite directions. Stitch and press. Repeat this process to make four sets.

4. Place two sets of eight blocks right sides together with seam allowances facing in opposite directions. Stitch and press. Repeat this process with the other set. (Figure 8)

5. Trim the Sixteen Patch blocks to measure exactly 9½" square.

ADDING THE SASHING

1. Lay out the quilt top as you desire, using the Quilt Layout (page 99) as a reference. Place the blocks six across and seven down, leaving about a 3" space between each block for sashing strips.

2. Place sashing strips between each block, between the rows and all around the outside.

3. Place a corner square at the intersection of each sashing. (Figure 9)

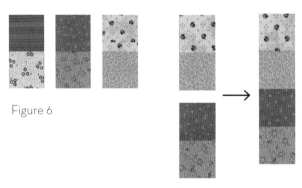

Figure 6

Figure 7

Figure 8

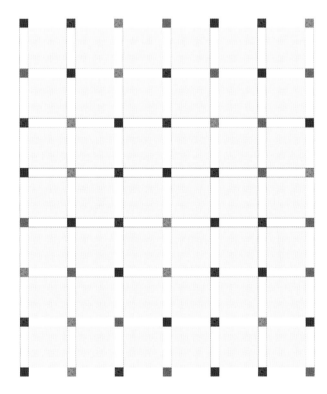

Figure 9

Sew You Know . . .

Depending on your fabrics, you have many options when making the Four Patch blocks. You may pair a dark pair with a light pair, a solid pair with a print pair, even a warm pair (yellow, orange and red) with a cool pair (green, blue and purple). The choices are up to you!

4. Starting with the first sashing row, stitch the corner blocks and sashing strips together. Press the seams toward the sashing strips. (Figure 10)

5. Stitch the first row of sashing strips to the blocks. Press the seams toward the sashing strips. (Figure 11)

6. Continue assembling the quilt rows as in steps 4 and 5, ending with the last sashing row.

7. Stitch the rows together to complete the inner quilt top, pressing as you go.

ADDING THE BORDER

1. To add each side border, measure the quilt from top to bottom in several places. Average the results and cut two border strips that length. Attach one strip to each side of the quilt. Press the seams toward this border.

2. Measure the quilt from side to side in several places. Average the results and cut the remaining two border strips that length. Attach these strips to the top and bottom of the quilt. Press the seams toward this border.

Layer and quilt, bind and enjoy!

Figure 10

Figure 11

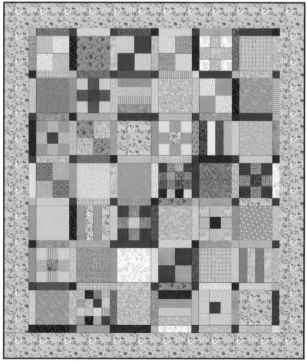

Alternate Colorway

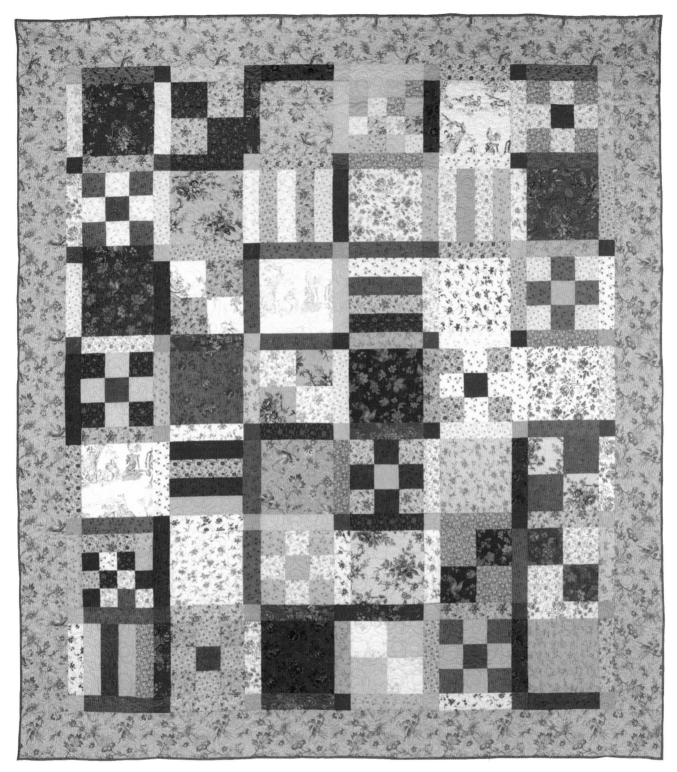

Quilt Layout

VARIATIONS:
Big Brother's Quilt + Kid Sister's Quilt

You know I have to get my grandchildren in here somewhere! Xavier is a big boy and needs a big-boy quilt, and his precious little Guenivere is outgrowing her crib! This pair of quilts is a variation of *PRE-CUTS POTPOURRI* (page 94). I added a few triangles and then divided the fabric up into two quilts.

Big Brother Size: 86" × 97" (Double/Queen)

Kid Sister Size: 64" × 75" (Throw)

Block Size: 9" × 9"

Fabric: *Max and Whiskers* by Moda

Pieced by the author, quilted by Bobbi Lang.

Kid Sister's Quilt Layout

This Quilt's Pre-Cuts...

layer cake • charm squares •
jelly roll • turnover

MATERIALS

FOR PRE-CUTS QUILT

1 layer cake (Blocks)

40 pairs of identical 5" charm squares, for a total of 80 squares (Blocks)

1 jelly roll (Blocks)

1 turnover (Blocks)

Additional yardage

FOR FAT QUARTER QUILT

1 fat quarter bundle or at least 40 fat quarters of a fabric line for blocks

Additional yardage

ADDITIONAL YARDAGE

KID SISTER:

⅓ yd. orange fabric (Border 1)
2 yds. coordinating fabric (Border 3 and Binding)

BIG BROTHER:

⅜ yd. black fabric (Border 1)
2⅝ yds. coordinating fabric (Border 3 and Binding)

BATTING AND BACKING YARDAGE

Twin and queen size battings (pieced from length to widen)

Backing (choose one):

42" wide fabric: KS: 4 yds./ BB: 7⅝ yds.

90" wide fabric: KS: 2 yds./ BB: 2⅞ yds.

108" wide fabric: KS: 2 yds./ BB: 2⅔ yds.

CUTTING INSTRUCTIONS

For Fat Quarter Quilts Only

Using the Fat Quarter Cutting Diagram as a guide, cut from each fat quarter:

(3) 2½" wide jelly roll strips.

(1) 10" wide layer cake strip; subcut into (1) 10" square.

(1) horizontal charm square strip 5" × 10"; subcut into (2) 5" squares.

(1) 6" strip; subcut (1) 6" square; subcut square once diagonally into (2) half-square triangles.

Follow the instructions below for subcutting pre-cuts and cutting additional yardage.

For Both Pre-Cuts and Fat Quarter Quilts

For both the pre-cuts and fat quarter quilts, follow the cutting instructions for *PRE-CUTS POTPOURRI* (page 94) except as follows:

From the jelly roll:

Separate out 3 of the solid and tone-on-tone fabrics. From these fabrics, cut out (48) 2½" squares for sashing corner squares.

From the remaining jelly roll strips, cut out at least (146) 2½" × 9½" strips for sashing. From the 4" left of each strip, cut 38 more 2½" squares for sashing corners.

From the Border 1 yardage:

For *KID SISTER*, cut (6) 1½" strips.

For *BIG BROTHER*, cut (8) 1½" strips.

From the Border 3/Binding yardage:

For either quilt, cut (4) 6½" wide strips by the length of the fabric for Border 3.

For either quilt, cut 2½" strips for binding.

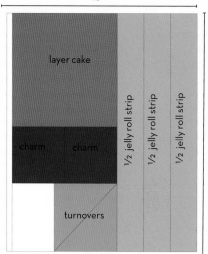

Fat Quarter Cutting Diagram

Sew You Know . . .

This pair of quilts also works well for twins. Instead of proportioning the quilts smaller and larger, just make them the same size!

SEWING INSTRUCTIONS

These instructions will make enough blocks for both quilts. Following the Sewing Instructions for *PRE-CUTS POTPOURRI* (pages 96–97), make all the blocks in that quilt. Then make ten Pinwheel blocks as follows:

1. Mixing and matching your turnover triangles, join them along the long edges to make square blocks. Press all the seams in the same direction. (Figure 1)

2. Randomly combine four of these blocks to create each Pinwheel block. As you lay out the blocks, be sure that all the diagonal seams meet in the middle of the pinwheel. Press. (Figure 2)

3. Trim these blocks to 9½" square, being sure to position a diagonal seam in each corner.

ADDING THE SASHING

Lay out the quilt tops as desired, using the Quilt Layouts (pages 100, 103) as a reference. Place the blocks four across by five down (*KID SISTER*), and six across by seven down (*BIG BROTHER*). Leave about a 3" space between each block for sashing strips.

Follow the rest of the sashing instructions in *PRE-CUTS POTPOURRI* (pages 97–98).

ADDING THE BORDERS

Border 1

1. To add the side borders to either quilt, measure the quilt from top to bottom in several places and average the results. Piece and cut two border strips that length. Attach one strip to each side of the quilt. Press the seams toward this border.

2. Measure the quilt from side to side in several places and average the results. Piece and cut the remaining two border strips that length. Attach these strips to the top and bottom of the quilt. Press the seams toward this border.

Border 2 (Optional Pieced Border)

1. Gather together all the leftover pieces from your quilt top so far. Cut as many as you can into 1" strips. Join the strips together and crosscut into 2½" units. Join these units until you have enough to make borders. (Figure 3)

2. Measure your quilt as you did for Border 1 and cut the pieced strips accordingly. Attach them to the quilt as you did for Border 1.

Border 3

In the same manner as you used for Border 1, measure and sew the 6" border strips to complete the quilt top.

Layer and quilt, bind and enjoy!

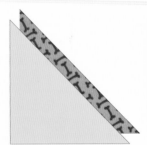

Figure 1

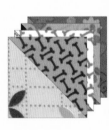

Figure 2

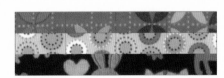

Figure 3

Sew You Know . . .

You will notice that I divided up the colors too, to make one more orange and brown and the other more turquoise and black. Depending on your fabric selection, you can make quilts customized for all the children in your life!

Big Brother's Quilt Layout

Rudolph's Encouragement Committee

Sometimes we all need a little encouragement from our friends, and I'm sure Rudolph was no exception! Have you ever wondered how you can take just about any adorable panel and make it into a fabulous quilt? With pre-cuts, it's all about easy borders!

Quilt Size: $62\frac{1}{2}$" × $72\frac{1}{2}$" (Throw/Twin)

Panel Size: 22" × $31\frac{1}{2}$"

Pieced and quilted by Wendy Russell.

Choosing Fabrics

I used the *Crazy Eights* Moda pre-cut line for this quilt. Every year Moda and other fabric makers introduce lines of pre-cuts with panels that you can easily adapt to this pattern. Or use any line that has a spectrum of country Christmas colors. Purchase additional yardage as specified in colors that coordinate with your particular pre-cut line.

- -

This Quilt's Pre-Cuts...

panel • charm squares • dessert roll • turnover • jelly roll

MATERIALS

FOR PRE-CUTS QUILT

1 panel

(44) 5" charm squares

1 dessert roll of (10) 5" tone-on-tone strips or ⅛ yd. each of 4 tone-on-tone fabrics

1 turnover

1 jelly roll

Additional yardage

FOR FAT QUARTER QUILT

1 panel

1 fat quarter bundle or at least 25 coordinating fat quarters

Additional yardage

ADDITIONAL YARDAGE

1½ yds. red print fabric

BATTING AND BACKING YARDAGE

Twin size batting

Backing (choose one):

42" wide fabric: 3¾ yds.
90" wide fabric: 2 yds.
108" wide fabric: 2 yds.

CUTTING INSTRUCTIONS

For Fat Quarter Quilt Only

Using the Fat Quarter Cutting Diagram as a guide, cut:

(2) 2½" wide jelly roll strips.

(1) 5" wide dessert roll strip.

(1) 6" wide horizontal turnover strip; subcut into (1) 6 square; subcut squares once diagonally from corner to corner. Subcut the rest of the strip into 5" charm squares.

Follow the instructions below for subcutting pre-cuts and cutting additional yardage.

For Pre-Cuts and Fat Quarter Quilts

Trim the panel to 22½" wide by 32" long.

From the dessert roll, cut:

(1) 5" square from each color for Border 3 (you will need 4 colors).

(2) 4¼" wide strips for the Border 2 sides, and (2) 4" wide strips for the Border 2 top and bottom.

From the jelly roll:

Cut each pre-cut jelly roll strip in half, resulting in 21" strips. Divide them into 2 equal piles, one half of each strip in each pile, and set one pile aside for Border 7.

To make the binding, cut random lengths from the other pile, varying in length from 9"–12" until you have a total of about 300".

From the red print fabric, cut:

(3) 1½" strips for Border 1.

(5) 2¾" strips for Border 4.

(7) 2½" strips for Border 6.

(1) 5" strip subcut into 4 squares for Border 5.

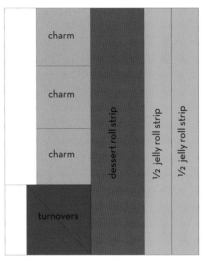

18"

22"

charm

charm

charm

turnovers

dessert roll strip

½ jelly roll strip

½ jelly roll strip

Fat Quarter Cutting Diagram

Sew You Know . . .

If you are using a panel from another fabric line, trim it down to 22½" × 32". If it is smaller than that, add strips to frame it and bring it up to that size. Some panels, like the one I used, have small blocks attached. Trim them to 5" square and use them in place of some charm squares.

SEWING INSTRUCTIONS

Border 1 (Red Print)

1. From the 1½" red print fabric strips, cut two 32" long strips. Sew one to each side of the panel. Press the seams toward the border.

2. Piece together and cut two 24½" red print strips. Sew them to the top and bottom of the panel. Press the seams toward the border. (Figure 1)

Border 2 (Dessert Roll)

1. Cut the two 4¼" wide strips to 34" long. Sew them to each side of the quilt. Press the seams toward this border.

2. Cut the two 4" wide strips to 32" long . Sew them to the top and bottom of the quilt. Press the seams toward this border. (Figure 2)

3. Your quilt should now measure 32" × 41".

Border 3 (Charm Squares and Turnovers)

1. Choose twenty-four light and twenty-four dark turnovers to make half-square triangles. Pair each light with a dark and stitch along the long diagonal edge, right sides together. Open up the squares and press the seams open. (Figure 3)

2. Trim the half-square triangles to exactly 5" square, making sure that the seams are exactly in opposite corners.

3. Using the four 5" squares from your dessert roll, eight 5" squares cut from your panel or additional yardage, and twenty-four turnover squares from step 2, assemble the border. Stitch the blocks together using Figure 4 as a guide. Press.

4. Sew the side borders to each side of the quilt. Press the seams toward Border 2.

5. The top and bottom borders include the corner blocks. Sew these borders to the top and bottom of the quilt. Press the seams toward Border 2. (Figure 4)

6. Your quilt should now measure 41" × 50".

Figure 1

Figure 2

Figure 3

Figure 4

Border 4 (Red Print)

1. From the 2¾" red print fabric, piece together and cut two 50" long strips. Sew one to each side of the quilt. Press the seams toward this border.

2. Piece together and cut two 45½" long strips. Sew them to the top and bottom of the quilt. Press toward this border. (Figure 5)

3. Your quilt should now measure 45½" x 54½".

Border 5 (Charm Squares)

1. Gather forty-four 5" charm squares and the four red print corner squares.

2. Each side border is made of twelve charm squares. Stitch them together, pressing seams in one direction. Sew the borders to the sides of the quilt. Press the seams toward Border 4.

3. The top and bottom borders have twelve charm squares each, beginning and ending with a red fabric square. Sew them together, pressing seams in one direction. Sew the borders to the top and bottom of the quilt. Press the seams toward Border 4. (Figure 6)

4. Your quilt should measure 54½" × 63½".

Border 6 (Red Fabric)

1. Sew two 2½" wide strips end-to-end to make a strip about 84" long. Repeat with the other two strips. Press the seams. Cut both strips 63½" long. Sew one to each side of the quilt. Press the seams toward this border.

2. Sew two of the short 3" wide strips to the ends of the two long 3" wide strips to make a strip about 63" long. Repeat with the other two strips. Press the seams. Cut the strips into two 58½" long strips. Sew them to the top and bottom of the quilt. Press the seams toward this border. (Figure 7)

Figure 5

Figure 6

Figure 7

Border 7 (Jelly Roll Squares)

1. Using the stack of 21" long jelly roll strips, pair up nine dark strips with nine light strips. If you do not have an even number of each, that is okay; just do not pair up two similar fabrics. You will also need two 2½" squares cut from leftover yardage.

2. With right sides together, strip piece the jelly roll strip pairs together along one long side. Press the seams toward the darker color. (Figure 8)

3. Crosscut the strips into 2½" units. (Figure 9)

4. Mixing up all the units, join them end-to-end into strips to make the borders. You will have thirty-four squares or seventeen units in each of the side borders. You will have thirty-one squares or fifteen units plus one extra square in each top and bottom border. These include the corner squares. (Figure 10)

5. Stitch the side borders to each side of the quilt. Press the seams toward Border 6.

6. Stitch the top and bottom borders to the quilt. Press the seams toward Border 6.

Layer and quilt, bind and enjoy!

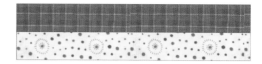

Figure 8

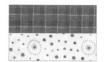

Figure 9

Figure 10

Alternate Colorway

Quilt Layout

Christmas Blessing

The icons of Christmas need no words. This little quilt brings the message of Christmas in a simple package of dessert roll strips and foundation-pieced blocks. You will find plenty of room on this wall hanging to showcase your very favorite quilting patterns.

Quilt Size: 27½" × 45½" (Wall Hanging)

Block Size: 9" × 9"

Pieced and quilted by the author.

Choosing Fabrics

I used the *Figgy Pudding* Moda pre-cut line for this quilt. If it's not available, choose pre-cuts that feature country Christmas colors with a focus on greens, reds and golds. Or use any line of contrasting colors. Purchase additional yardage as specified in colors that coordinate with your particular pre-cut line.

- -

This Quilt's Pre-Cuts...

dessert roll • charm squares • honey bun

MATERIALS

FOR PRE-CUTS QUILT

1 dessert roll of (10) 5" tone-on-tone strips or ⅙ yd. each of 10 coordinating tone-on-tone fabrics

(42) 5" charm squares

1 honey bun

FOR FAT QUARTER QUILT

1 fat quarter bundle or at least 12 coordinating fat quarters

⅙ yd. each of 10 tone-on-tone fabrics

BATTING AND BACKING YARDAGE

Crib size batting

Backing (choose one):

42" wide fabric: 1½ yds.
90" wide fabric: 1 yd.
108" wide fabric: 1 yd.

EXTRA SUPPLIES

Foundation piecing paper

Foundation patterns (pages 123–124)

CUTTING INSTRUCTIONS

For Fat Quarter Quilt Only

Using the Fat Quarter Cutting Diagram as a guide, cut from each fat quarter:

(1) 5" wide charm square strip; subcut into 5" squares.

(8) 1½" wide honey bun strips.

From the 10 tone-on-tone fabrics:

Cut each fabric to a 5" wide strip.

For Pre-Cuts and Fat Quarter Quilts

From the dessert roll, cut:

(1) 41" long red no. 1 strip for top horizontal Border.

(1) 23" long red no. 2 strip for left vertical Border.

(1) 36½" long brown no. 1 strip for bottom horizontal Border.

(1) 27½" long brown no. 2 strip for right vertical Border.

(1) 27½" long strip and (1) 5" square from both a blue and white dessert roll strip for sky and ground.

(1) 9½" long strip and (1) 5" square from both green no. 1 and green no. 2.

Cut the remaining dessert roll strips in half lengthwise into 2½" wide strips. Set aside approximately 160" of various colors and lengths for binding.

Use the remaining fabric as needed for foundation piecing.

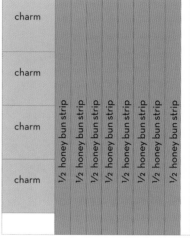

Fat Quarter Cutting Diagram

SEWING INSTRUCTIONS

1. Copy the foundation patterns onto the foundation paper, remembering to reverse the pattern. Be sure each block is exactly 9" square plus the outside ¼" seam allowances.

2. Using your preferred method of foundation piecing, construct the three blocks using the enlarged patterns from pages 123–124. Choose colors that provide good contrast between each part of the block (roof, walls, sky, windows, etc.).

3. After each block is finished, stitch around the outer edges within the ¼" seam allowance. Remove all the paper.

Sew You Know . . .

BASIC FOUNDATION PIECING METHOD

1. Cut a piece of fabric ½" larger all around than the A1 section of the enlarged foundation pattern (pages 123–124). Do the same with a different fabric for the A2 section.

2. Turn the foundation pattern wrong-side up. With right sides together, place the two fabrics over the A1 section, with two edges overlapping the line between the A1 and A2 spaces by approximately ¼". Pin the fabrics along that line. Open up the top fabric and fold it back to ensure it thoroughly covers the A2 space with at least ¼" extra on all sides. Return the fabric to wrong-side-up position and pin in place. (Figure A)

3. Turn the pattern with pinned fabrics over so you are working with the printed side up. With a short stitch, sew along the solid line between A1 and A2. Trim the fabric to a scant ¼" seam allowance. Press the top fabric open and pin it in place. (Figure B)

4. Repeat to sew a piece of fabric to cover the A3 spot by placing the A3 fabric right sides together with A2 and continuing on as explained above. (Figure C)

5. Continue to sew the entire foundation pattern. (Figure D)

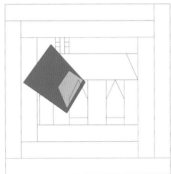

Figure A

Figure B

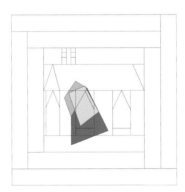

Figure C

Figure D

ASSEMBLING THE QUILT TOP

1. With right sides together, match up the lower left corner of the Church block and the lower right corner of the 5" green no. 2 square. Sew a vertical seam about 2" up the side. Press open. (Figure 1)

2. With right sides together, match up the upper right corner of the House block and the upper left corner of the 5" green no. 1 square. Sew a vertical seam about 2" down the side. Press open. (Figure 2)

3. Join the 5" blue square to the left end of the 9½" green no. 1 strip. Press. (Figure 3)

4. Join the white 5" square to the right end of the 9½" green no. 2 strip. Press. (Figure 4)

5. With right sides together, attach the bottom edge of the Church block to the top edge of the green/white unit. Press. (Figure 5)

6. With right sides together, attach the top edge of the House block to the bottom edge of the green/blue unit. Press. (Figure 6)

Figure 1

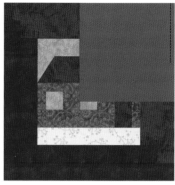
Figure 2

Figure 3

Figure 4

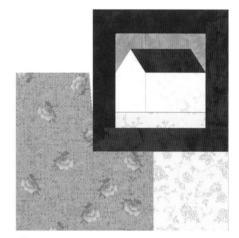
Figure 5

Figure 6

Sew You Know . . .

Pre-cuts are a natural choice for foundation piecing because they are already smaller sizes. As you proceed, just cut the best-fitting pre-cuts into smaller, more workable pieces.

7. With right sides together, attach the Church block from step 5 to the right side of the Tree block and the House block from step 6 to the left side of the Tree block. Press. (Figure 7)

8. With right sides together, attach the blue sky strip to the top of the Tree/House unit, and the white ground strip to the bottom of the Tree/Church unit. Press. (Figure 8)

9. With right sides together, finish the seams from steps 1 and 2 to enclose the left side of the Church block and the right side of the House block. Press. (Figure 9)

10. With right sides together, sew the brown no. 1 border to the bottom of the quilt. Press.

11. With right sides together, sew the red no. 2 border to the left side of the quilt. Press.

12. With right sides together, sew the red no. 1 border to the top of the quilt. Press.

13. With right sides together, sew the brown no. 2 border to the right side of the quilt. Press.

Quilt, bind and enjoy!

Figure 7

Figure 8

Figure 9

Alternate Colorway

Quilt Layout

Pre-Cuts Inspiration Gallery

Musky Dusky Woods
Pieced by the author,
quilted by Bobbi Lang.

Chasing Windmills
in the Orchard
Pieced by the author,
quilted by Bobbi Lang.

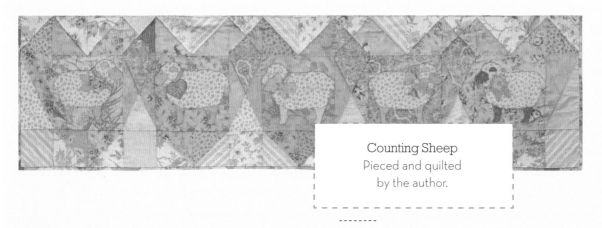

Counting Sheep
Pieced and quilted
by the author.

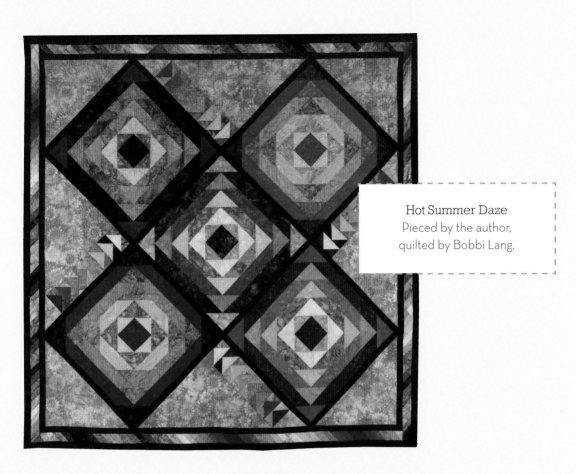

Hot Summer Daze
Pieced by the author,
quilted by Bobbi Lang.

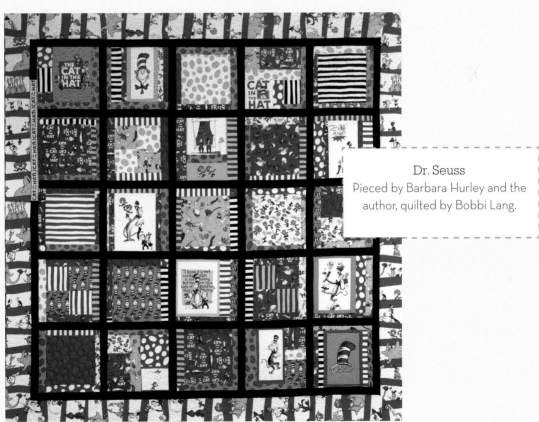

Dr. Seuss
Pieced by Barbara Hurley and the
author, quilted by Bobbi Lang.

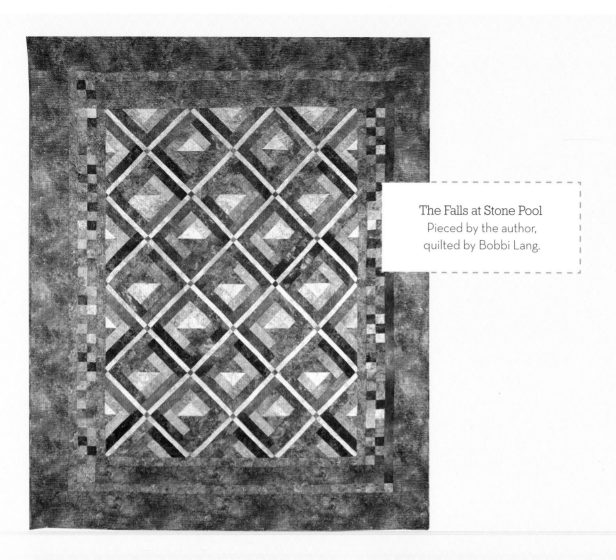

The Falls at Stone Pool
Pieced by the author,
quilted by Bobbi Lang.

I Love This Quilt!
Pieced by the author,
quilted by Bobbi Lang.

The Softer Side of Spring
Pieced by the author,
quilted by Bobbi Lang.

The Fall of Autumn
Pieced by the author,
quilted by Bobbi Lang.

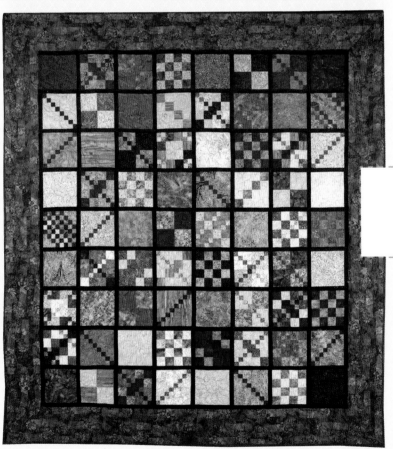

The Gems of Bali
Pieced by the author,
quilted by Bobbi Lang.

Patterns + Templates

Carefully enlarge each pattern or template at the indicated percentage before tracing and cutting out the shape.

Wonky Posies
4½" Large Petal Template
Shown at 50%. Enlarge at 200%.

Wonky Posies
Rounded Corners Edge Template
Shown at 50%. Enlarge at 200%.

Wonky Posies
3¼" Small Petal Template
Shown at 50%. Enlarge at 200%.

Wonky Posies
Focus Corner Template
Shown at 25%. Enlarge at 200%;
then enlarge at 200% again.

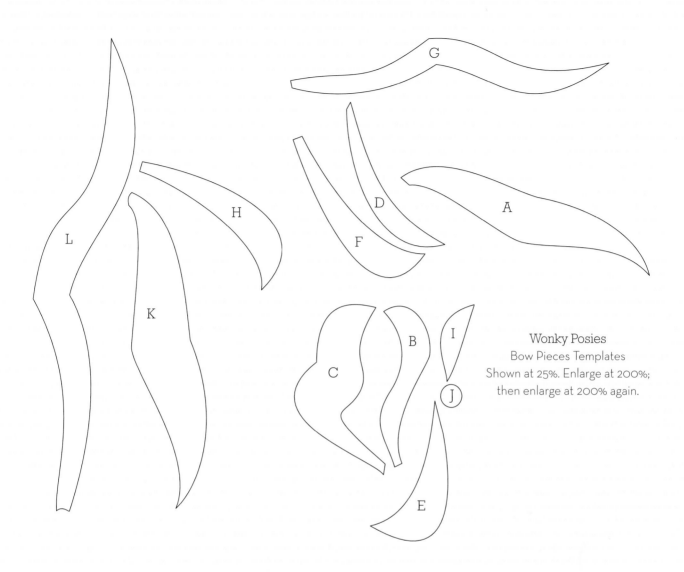

Wonky Posies
Bow Pieces Templates
Shown at 25%. Enlarge at 200%;
then enlarge at 200% again.

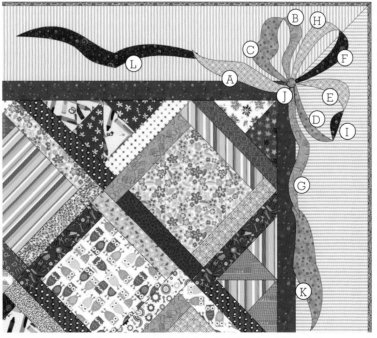

Bow Placement Guide

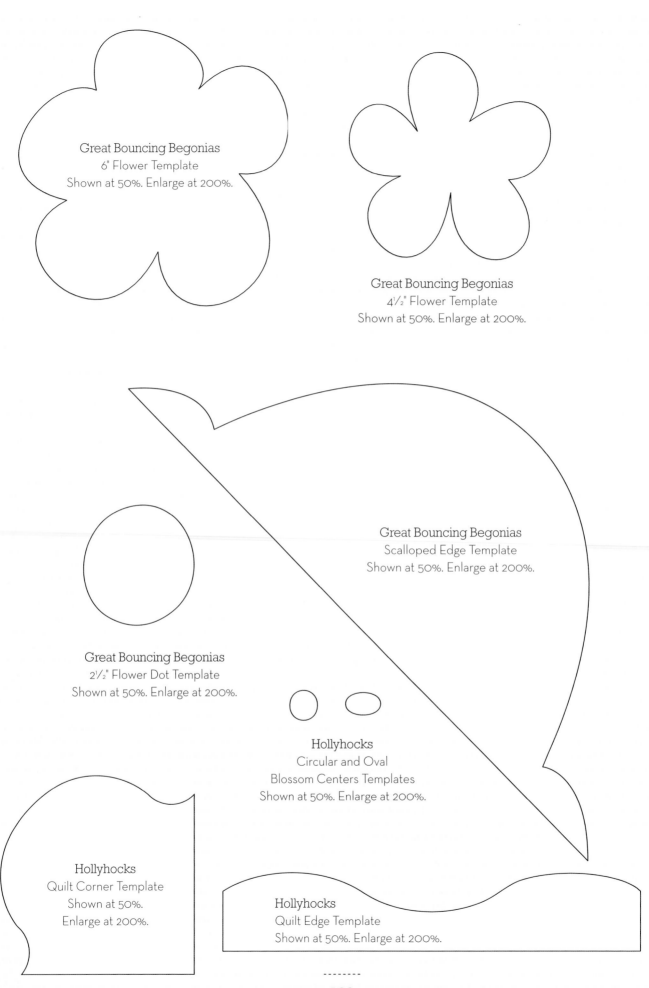

Great Bouncing Begonias
6" Flower Template
Shown at 50%. Enlarge at 200%.

Great Bouncing Begonias
4½" Flower Template
Shown at 50%. Enlarge at 200%.

Great Bouncing Begonias
Scalloped Edge Template
Shown at 50%. Enlarge at 200%.

Great Bouncing Begonias
2½" Flower Dot Template
Shown at 50%. Enlarge at 200%.

Hollyhocks
Circular and Oval
Blossom Centers Templates
Shown at 50%. Enlarge at 200%.

Hollyhocks
Quilt Corner Template
Shown at 50%.
Enlarge at 200%.

Hollyhocks
Quilt Edge Template
Shown at 50%. Enlarge at 200%.

Hollyhocks
Small, Medium and Large Leaf and Blossom Templates
Shown at 50%. Enlarge at 200%.

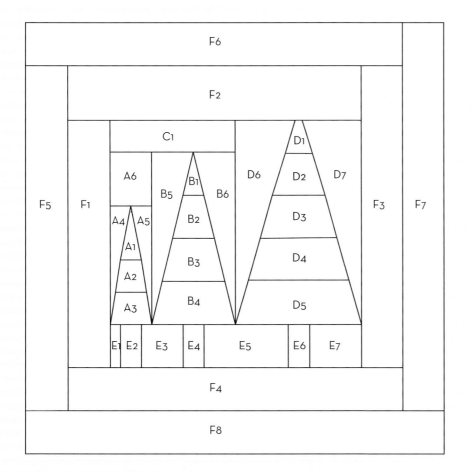

Christmas Blessings
Trees Foundation Pattern
Shown at 50%. Enlarge at 200%.

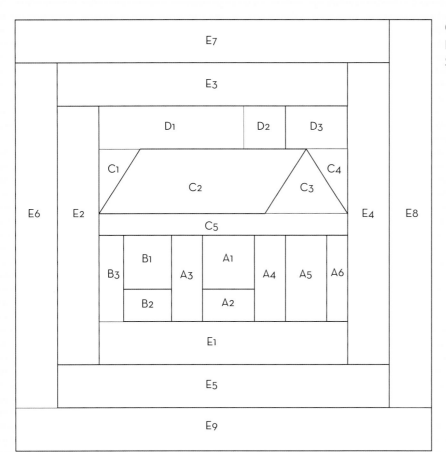

Christmas Blessings
House Foundation Pattern
Shown at 50%. Enlarge at 200%.

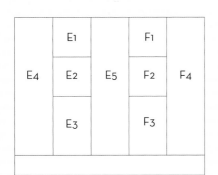

Steeple Piecing
Diagram Enlarged

Christmas Blessings
Church Foundation Pattern
Shown at 50%. Enlarge at 200%.

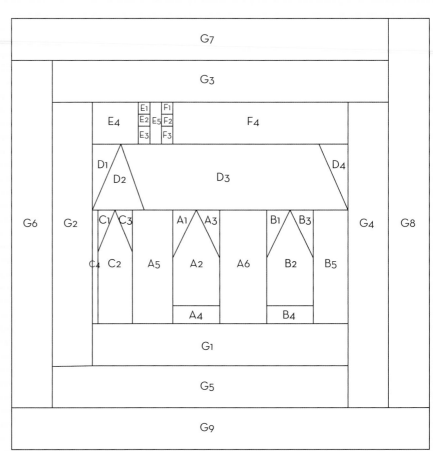

Index

ACKNOWLEDGMENTS & DEDICATION

"Now unto the King eternal, immortal, invisible, the only wise God, be honour and glory for ever and ever. Amen." (1 Tim. 1:17 KJV)

- In loving memory of Matilda Wanner Gerber and Salome Ifft Fehr—Tilly and Sally, grammas who first inspired me.
- I dedicate this book to Tate, my beloved husband, who stood by me and sacrificed to make it happen. I love you! Every orange fabric is for you.
- Our daughters, Amy Greenway and April Greenway-Horsman, both amazing, accomplished, loving young women of whom I am just dizzyingly proud.
- Xavier Cade and Guenivere Rain: grandchildren. That says it all!
- Eugene and Margaret Fehr: Mom and Dad, who still believe I'm capable of anything and are probably wondering what will be next.
- Brothers 3: Den, Terry and Jay, the loves of a truly great family.
- And oh, my quilting friends! How could I have done it without you?
- My good old friends from Washington Square Quilters' Guild, Washington, Illinois: Debi Henninger, who opened the door for me with *Hobo Quilts* and made precious memories! Wendy Russell, who stitched through her grief in losing her beloved Jim to see my project through. I love you, most lofty friend. Claudette Cremer, you amaze me with your absolutely persnickety perfect work. Barbara Hurley, Diana Snyder, Susan Wozniak, Janet Wylie—I do so appreciate you and love the projects! And Sew You Know . . ., Val Williams!
- My good new friends from Waldron and Belle Point Quilt Guild of Fort Smith, Arkansas: Philis Cook, you bind like a lightning flash. Phyllis Housch, thank you for adopting me down there; your guidance is so valuable. Reita Plummer, my car poolie, thank you for showing me around and pitching in to get it done. Finally, Bobbi Lang, you are an angel straight from heaven. I honestly could not have done it without you.
- The ever-helpful gang at Electric Quilt Software: you rock!
- Kelly Biscopink, my editor: I put you at the bottom, not because you are the least, but because you supported the whole bunch of us. You are amazing! I could not have asked for a better, more tireless or patient editor.

ABOUT THE AUTHOR

I remember my first quilt—don't we all? I was in high school and made it from children's hankies. It could have been so cute! I still pull it out once in a while when I need a smile.

My grandmothers were accomplished needle workers, and watching them always fascinated me. My mom made sure I understood that the doll clothes or sweaters they made were very special and something to treasure. So I did. Growing up with an appreciation of my dad's art and loving parents who encouraged my own talents laid a foundation for which I shall forever be thankful. My parents are truly the greatest!

I met my husband, Tate, at work when I lived in Tucson, Arizona. (Thankfully, I snapped him up before I caught the quilting bug.) We settled on a beautiful plot of land in the high desert to raise our precious little family, a few pet chickens, some blackberries and a miserable garden!

I dabbled with many needle arts until the mid-1980s when I caught the quilting epidemic that swept the country and the world. I still managed to graduate from the University of Arizona with a degree in interpersonal communication, and then we moved to Denver, Colorado, for seminary. Even then I'd sneak down the street to the local quilt shop for a break now and then. Finally, we moved to Illinois to be near my parents until our daughters were out of school.

I worked and taught for years at Peg and Lil's Needlepatch in Washington, Illinois, and then more years for Peddler's Way Quilt Company when Lillian retired.

After some time off to play gramma, I joined Debi Henninger as administrative assistant to her three shops in Metamora, Pekin and Peoria, Illinois. That's when Debi's *Hobo Quilts* came about, and I knew I had to write a book, too. I was hooked! Krause Publications took me into their fold and well, here I am. In 2010, on New Year's Day, we temporarily "retired" to small-town Waldron, Arkansas, where I saw this book dream come true. Then it was back to central Illinois for the next chapter of our lives. What a journey!

media
www.fwmedia.com

16 15 14 13 12   5 4 3 2 1

DISTRIBUTED IN CANADA BY FRASER DIRECT
100 Armstrong Avenue
Georgetown, ON, Canada L7G 5S4
Tel: (905) 877-4411

DISTRIBUTED IN THE U.K. AND EUROPE BY F&W MEDIA
INTERNATIONAL
Brunel House, Newton Abbot, Devon, TQ12 4PU, England
Tel: (+44) 1626 323200, Fax: (+44) 1626 323319
Email: enquiries@fwmedia.com

DISTRIBUTED IN AUSTRALIA BY CAPRICORN LINK
P.O. Box 704, S. Windsor NSW, 2756 Australia
Tel: (02) 4577-3555

SRN: W0708
ISBN-13: 978-1-4402-1731-9

Editor: Kelly Biscopink

Designer: Megan Richards

Production Coordinator:
Greg Nock

Photographer: Christine
Polomsky

Photo Stylist: Lauren
Emmerling

Metric Conversion Chart

To convert	to	multiply by
Inches	Centimeters	2.54
Centimeters	Inches	0.4
Feet	Centimeters	30.5
Centimeters	Feet	0.03
Yards	Meters	0.9
Meters	Yards	1.1

Inches to Centimeters Conversion Chart

¼ in	6mm	6½ in	16.5cm	14½ in	36.8cm	22½ in	57.2cm
½ in	1.3cm	7 in	17.8cm	15 in	38.1cm	23 in	58.4cm
¾ in	1.9cm	7½ in	19.1cm	15½ in	39.4cm	23½ in	59.7cm
1 in	2.5cm	8 in	20.3cm	16 in	40.6cm	24 in	61cm
1¼ in	3.2cm	8½ in	21.6cm	16½ in	41.9cm	24½ in	62.2cm
1½ in	3.8cm	9 in	22.9cm	17 in	43.2cm	25 in	63.5cm
1¾ in	4.4cm	9½ in	24.1cm	17½ in	44.5cm	25½ in	64.8cm
2 in	5.1cm	10 in	25.4cm	18 in	45.7cm	26 in	66cm
2½ in	6.4cm	10½ in	26.7cm	18½ in	47cm	26½ in	67.3cm
3 in	7.6cm	11 in	27.9cm	19 in	48.3cm	27 in	68.6cm
3½ in	8.9cm	11½ in	29.2cm	19½ in	49.5cm	27½ in	69.9cm
4 in	10.2cm	12 in	30.5cm	20 in	50.8cm	28 in	71.1cm
4½ in	11.4cm	12½ in	31.8cm	20½ in	52.1cm	28½ in	72.4cm
5 in	12.7cm	13 in	33cm	21 in	53.3cm	29 in	73.7cm
5½ in	14cm	13½ in	34.3cm	21½ in	54.6cm	29½ in	74.9cm
6 in	15.2cm	14 in	35.6cm	22 in	55.9cm	30 in	76.2cm

DISCOVER THESE TITLES *for more*
fast and fun quilt projects!

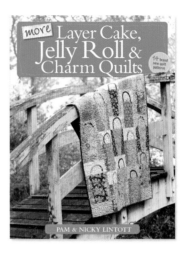

3-Fabric Quilts
by Leni Levenson Wiener

In *3-Fabric Quilts*, Leni Levenson Wiener gives you the tools to make twelve fantastic quilts, each requiring only three fabrics. You'll get helpful advice on choosing the three fabrics, including tips on understanding color, value and print scale. Illustrated instructions for twelve quilts, each with yardage requirements and instructions for a small and large size, make quilting fun, whether you're a beginner or advanced quilter. With a few simple tricks and tips, choose just three fabrics and be on your way to a fabulous finished quilt!

More Layer Cake, Jelly Roll and Charm Quilts
by Pam and Nicky Lintott

Pam and Nicky Lintott have sold over 250,000 books all over the world—a testament to their extraordinary talent for creating great quilt designs with easy-to-follow instructions. Here Pam and Nicky bring you a fresh collection of fourteen brand new quilt patterns, each with a beautiful variation design. Use a range of Moda™ pre-cuts, including the new fat eighth bundle!

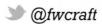